THE REMIX GENERATION

Is Everything a Repeat?

By

Eric Buffett

Copyright 2024, Eric Buffett. All rights reserved. No portion of this book may be reproduced in any form or by any electronic or mechanical means, including information storage and retrieval systems, without prior written permission from the publisher, with the exception of reviewers who may quote brief passages in their reviews.

Copyright © 2024

Table of Contents

Preface

Introduction:

The Message Is in the Remix

➢ Defining the concept of "remix" in a broad cultural context.

➢ Examining the Folklore, Literature, and Art Historical Foundations of Remixing Outside of Digital Technology

➢ Setting the stage for the central question: Is everything a remix?

➢ Overview of the book's structure and key arguments.

Chapter 1:

Echoes of the Past: Pre-Digital Remixing

1.1 Exploring examples of remixing in pre-digital eras:

1.2 Variations and Adaptations of Classical Music: A Tradition Before Digital Remix

1.3 Examining Retellings and Adaptations in Literature

1.4 The Development of Folk Music Through Oral Tradition

1.5 The Impact of Previous Artistic Movements on Later Ones

1.6 Establishing the continuity of remixing as a human creative practice.

Chapter 2:

The Digital Revolution: Tools of Transformation

2.1 Digital Technology's Emergence and Effect on Remixing

2.2 The Development of Digital Manipulation, Looping, and Sampling in Music

2.3 The Development of Digital Image Manipulation and Editing

2.4 The Internet as a Channel for Remixed Content Distribution and Sharing

2.5 Hardware and Software's Impact on Creative Potential

Chapter 3:

Copyright and Creativity: The Remix Dilemma

3.1 Examining the legal framework of copyright and its implications for remix culture.

3.2 The Argument Between Transformative and Fair Use

3.3 Examples of Copyright Conflicts Concerning Remixed Works

3.4 The Function of Alternative Licensing

Models, Including Creative Commons

3.5 The Conflict Between Encouraging Creativity and Preserving the Rights of Creators

Chapter 4:

Music Remixed: From Sampling to Mashups

4.1 Examining the Development and History of Music Remixing

4.2 Hip-hop and Electronic Music's Effect on Remix Culture

4.3 Examples of Famous Remixes and Their Cultural Influence

4.4 Mashups' Ascent and Importance in Remixing Classic Works

4.5 The Impact of Remixing on the Creation of Modern Music

Chapter 5:

Visual Culture Remixed: From Fan Art to Memes

5.1 Analyzing Remixing's Function in Visual Culture

5.2 The phenomenon of fan art, fan fiction, and other forms of fan-created content.

5.3 The Development of Internet Memes and Their Contribution to the Spread of Culture

5.4 The Application of Remixing in Marketing, Propaganda, and Advertising

5.5 Digital Manipulation's Effect on Photography and Video

Chapter 6:

Narrative Remixed: Retellings, Adaptations, and Transmedia Storytelling

6.1 Examining the Idea of Story Remixing in Film, Literature, and Other Media

6.2 The Function of Sequels, Remakes, and Adaptations in Continuing Current Storylines

6.3. Transmedia Storytelling's Development and Dependency on Cross-Platform Remixing

6.4 The impact of fan fiction and other forms of participatory culture on narrative remixing.

6.5 Examples from Literature, Video Games, Television, and Film

Chapter 7:

Identity Remixed: Self-Presentation in the Digital Age

7.1 Analyzing How People in the Digital Age Remix Their Identities

7.2 The role of social media in shaping online identities.

7.3 Using Profiles, Avatars, and Other Online Self-Representation Tools

7.4 The Idea of "Digital Selves" and How They

Connect to Actual Identities

7.5 Identity's Flexibility and Malleability in Online Environments

Chapter 8:

The Ethics of Remixing: Appropriation, Authorship, and Ownership

8.1 What Remix Culture Has to Offer in Terms of Ethics

8.2 The Argument Between Inspiration and Appropriation

8.3 The Ownership and Authorship Issue in Remixed Works

8.4 The Value of Citations and Attribution to Original Sources

8.5 Getting Around the Ethical Remixing Gray Areas

Chapter 9:

The Future of Remixing: AI, Algorithms, and Beyond

9.1 Examining the Possible Effects of Algorithms and Artificial Intelligence on Remixing

9.2 The Development of Generative AI and How It Affects Creative Production

9.3 Copyright and Intellectual Property's Future in an AI-Generated Content World

9.4 The Changing Interaction of Machines and Humans in Creative Processes

9.5 Hypotheses Regarding Upcoming Developments in Remix Culture

Conclusion:

Everything is a Remix? A nuanced Perspective

➢ Reexamining the Main Question: Is Everything a Remix?

➢ Is Everything a Remix? Asks the Remix Generation.

➢ Acknowledging the complexities and nuances of remix culture.

➢ Providing a Concluding View on the Character of Creativity and Originality in the Digital Age

Bibliography

Index

Is Everything a Remix? Asks the Remix Generation.

Preface

Within the creative sphere, where inspirations and ideas collide, there is an intriguing phenomenon called the *"Remix Generation."* This generation boldly embraces the art of reinterpretation, reimagining existing works to create something completely new, unconstrained by conventional ideas of originality. This generation is aware that creativity is more about deftly combining preexisting elements to create an innovative tapestry than it is about creating something entirely from scratch.

Remixing has been a fundamental component of human expression for centuries; it is not a new idea of the digital age. In order to produce their own original works of art, artists, musicians, writers, and thinkers have long looked to their forefathers for inspiration. But the rise of digital technology has expanded remixing's reach and accessibility, making it cultural phenomenon that influences every aspect of our lives.

The Remix Generation is distinguished by its voracious appetite for content, its adeptness at navigating the vast digital landscape, and its natural appreciation of the value of teamwork. This generation thrives on the sharing of ideas, the blending of different influences, and the coming together to create something truly remarkable.

This book, *"The Remix Generation,"* explores the roots, effects, and potential to influence the direction of creativity in order to get to the core of this cultural phenomenon. It looks at how remixing has changed a variety of fields, including literature, film, music, and art, and how it has changed how we think about authorship and ownership.

Get ready to learn from the perspectives and insights expressed by a wide range of voices as you set out on this intellectual adventure. This book is more than just a compilation of essays; it is a harmonious fusion of voices and a symphony of ideas that capture the essence of the Remix Generation.

I want to express my appreciation to the writers and contributors who have put their all into this project. Their commitment to examining the complex aspects of remixing has produced an educational and motivational piece.

I would also like to thank the readers who have decided to explore the remix generation with me. Your open-mindedness and curiosity are crucial to realizing the transformational potential of remixing.

I hope that this book will spark more discussion and investigation, encouraging us to embrace the Remix Generation's spirit and build a world where creativity is unrestricted.

Concerning the Writer

Renowned author and cultural analyst Eric Buffett has devoted his professional life to examining the relationship between creativity, technology, and society. He is known as a leading voice in the study of contemporary culture because of his perceptive observations and provocative analyses.

Buffett's writings have received a lot of praise for their ability to encapsulate the spirit of the digital age and illuminate the revolutionary forces that are changing the world. He is a sought-after speaker at conferences and events worldwide, and his writing has appeared in many publications.

Buffett continues his investigation into the dynamic realm of creativity with *"The Remix Generation,"* exploring the phenomenon of remixing and its significant cultural influence. This book is a must-read for anyone who wants to comprehend the forces influencing the future of creativity because of his perceptive analysis and captivating prose.

Introduction:

The Message Is in the Remix

Our world is a palimpsest, a multi-layered tapestry made from repurposed artifacts, reinterpreted stories, and borrowed concepts. Remixing—the act of taking preexisting elements and combining them in novel and unexpected ways—has been a fundamental driver of human creativity and cultural evolution since the earliest cave paintings, which echoed the forms of nature, to the most recent viral meme that riffed on current events. The book **"The Remix Generation: Is Everything a Remix?"** explores this widespread phenomenon's historical foundations, current expressions, and significant ramifications for our conceptions of originality, creativity, and authorship.

The central idea, which is summarized in the title of this introduction, **"The Remix is the Message,"** is based on Marshall McLuhan's well-known statement, *"The medium is the message."* According to McLuhan, a medium's form becomes a part of any message it transmits or conveys, forming a mutually reinforcing relationship in which the medium shapes the way the message is understood. The act of remixing itself takes center stage in 1 remix culture, displacing or, more accurately, recontextualizing the individual components being remixed. New interpretations and creative possibilities are sparked by the selection, combination, and transformation process, which turns into the center of meaning.

It's important to define *"remix"* in a broad cultural sense. Digital media manipulation is a major part of it, but it's not the only thing. Adaptation, appropriation, sampling, collage, pastiche, parody, and countless other creative reuse techniques are all included in the much broader category of remixing. It is evident in the literary tradition of recounting traditional myths and tales, in the artistic technique of collage, in the musical practice of varying a theme, and in the commonplace act of quoting and referencing.

Remixing's historical origins show that it is not a new phenomenon that emerged in the digital era. People were remixing their surroundings long before computers and the internet were invented. For instance, stories were constantly retold and modified in oral traditions, each time reflecting the unique context of the storyteller and their audience and introducing new levels of meaning. During the Middle Ages, architectural styles from earlier periods were reused and reinterpreted in the construction of cathedrals. Shakespeare created timeless pieces of dramatic art by heavily referencing pre-existing stories and historical accounts. These examples, along with numerous others, show how remixing is a basic part of human culture and how we communicate, learn, and create.

However, there is no denying that the digital revolution has increased the size and reach of remixing. Remixing has become a common cultural practice, and the process of creating content has become more accessible due to the ease with which digital content can be copied, altered, and shared. Anyone with a computer and an internet connection can now become a remixer thanks to software tools for text processing, image manipulation, and audio and video editing that have reduced the technical barriers to entry. The internet has developed into a huge, easily accessible library of sounds, pictures, and text that can be freely sampled and used for other purposes.

Because of its accessibility, thriving online communities devoted to remixing have emerged. Fan communities expand and reinterpret preexisting narratives and characters through the creation of fan fiction, fan art, and fan videos. Memes are a dynamic and constantly changing form of online communication that thrive on the quick spread and modification of images and phrases. In order to create new musical compositions that cross genres and eras, musicians sample and loop previously recorded music. These instances demonstrate how digital technologies can revolutionize a culture of remixing.

The main query this book attempts to answer is: Is everything a remix? Although it could be tempting to simply say *"**yes**"* in response to this question, the truth is much more complex. A reductive perspective that equates all creativity with simple copying should be avoided, even though it is true that all creative works are influenced by earlier works and that originality is frequently a matter of degree rather than absolute invention. Remixing is more than just copying; it also entails changing, rearranging, and adding new meaning. The ability to choose, blend, and work with preexisting elements to produce something truly original and perceptive is the remixer's skill.

The purpose of this book is to examine the different aspects of remix culture. To set the historical background, it looks at remixing in pre-digital forms. It explores how remixing practices are affected by digital technologies. It examines the moral and legal ramifications of remixing, especially as they pertain to intellectual property and copyright. It looks at particular instances of remixing in a variety of cultural fields, such as literature, visual art, music, and online culture. Additionally, it takes into account how remixing will develop in the era of algorithmic creativity and artificial intelligence.

This book aims to offer a framework for comprehending the intricate and varied aspects of remix culture rather than offering a conclusive response to the query of whether everything is a remix. We hope to shed light on the fundamental role that remixing plays in forming our creative landscape by examining its historical foundations, modern manifestations, and potential future developments. In all of its manifestations, the remix is more than just a technique; it is a powerful force for cultural innovation, a way of thinking, and a way of interacting with the outside world. The message is in the remix.

> ➤ **Defining the concept of "remix" in a broad cultural context**.

The word *"remix"* has become widely used in modern conversation, especially when talking about digital culture and artistic endeavors. But its significance goes well beyond the fields of video editing and music production. In order to define "remix" in a broad cultural context, it is necessary to recognize its historical origins, its varied applications in different fields, and its changing significance in a world that is changing quickly.

Fundamentally, a remix is the process of combining or changing preexisting elements—whether they be sounds, images, texts, ideas, or even cultural practices—to produce something new. Remix culture is characterized by this process of reusing and recontextualizing. Transforming and reinterpreting, adding new levels of meaning, and developing new forms of expression are more important than merely copying or reproducing.

Although the word *"remix"* became widely used as digital technologies advanced, the act of remixing is not new. Humans have used a variety of creative re-use techniques throughout history, modifying and reinterpreting preexisting works to fit their own period and setting. Important insights into the fundamental ideas of remix culture can be gained from these pre-digital remixing techniques.

For instance, it has long been customary in literature to retell and modify preexisting stories. Generation after generation has passed down myths, legends, and folk tales, each one with its own unique details and interpretations. Shakespeare is renowned for using pre-existing historical narratives and literary works as inspiration to create timeless plays. These adaptations are remixes that capture the aesthetic sensibilities and cultural values of their era, not just copies.

For centuries, a fundamental component of classical composition in music has been the use of variations on a theme. In order to experiment with various harmonies, rhythms, and instrumental textures, composers would take a basic melody and produce a number of variations. Remixing in a pre-digital era is exemplified by this process of reinterpreting a musical concept. The adaptation and reinterpretation of preexisting songs, with each performance incorporating new verses or melodic variations, is another common practice in folk music traditions.

One of the best examples of remixing in visual art is the collage technique, which combines various materials and images to create a new piece of art. Collage was first used in the early

20th century by artists such as Pablo Picasso and Georges Braque, who used found objects, fabric scraps, and newspaper clippings to create their paintings. One of the main components of remix culture is the method of contrasting different elements to produce new meaning.

The size and reach of remixing have greatly increased with the introduction of digital technologies. Remixing has become a common cultural practice, and the process of creating content has become more accessible due to the ease with which digital content can be copied, altered, and shared. Anyone with a computer and an internet connection can now become a remixer thanks to software tools for text processing, image manipulation, and audio and video editing that have reduced the technical barriers to entry.

The internet has developed into a huge, easily accessible library of sounds, pictures, and text that can be freely sampled and used for other purposes. Online communities devoted to remixing has grown as a result of the wealth of easily accessible content. Fan communities expand and reinterpret preexisting narratives and characters through the creation of fan fiction, fan art, and fan videos. Memes are a dynamic and constantly changing form of online communication that thrive on the quick spread and modification of images and phrases.

The word *"remix"* has acquired a specific meaning in the music industry, denoting the act of modifying an already existing recording by adding or deleting elements, altering the key or tempo, or adding new effects. Popular music production now heavily relies on this technique, especially in dance, electronic, and hip-hop genres. A crucial component of music remixing is sampling, a technique that entails fusing brief passages from pre-existing recordings into brand-new compositions.

The idea of remixing can be applied to a variety of cultural phenomena outside of these particular instances. Styles from earlier decades are frequently reinterpreted in fashion trends. Combining ingredients and methods from various culinary traditions is a common practice in culinary innovations. Even scientific breakthroughs can be viewed as a kind of remixing, expanding on preexisting theories and knowledge to produce fresh perspectives on the world.

Recognizing the ethical and legal ramifications of the term *"remix"* is also necessary when defining it in a broad cultural context. Important issues regarding authorship, ownership, and intellectual property are brought up by the remixing practice. Remixing and copyright law, which is intended to safeguard creators' rights, can occasionally clash, especially when using copyrighted content without authorization. When discussing remix culture, the idea of "fair use," which permits specific uses of copyrighted content without consent, is frequently brought up.

To sum up, defining the term "remix" in a broad cultural context necessitates acknowledging its historical origins, its varied applications in different fields, and its changing relevance in the digital era. Remixing is a cultural practice that embodies our fundamental human need to create, modify, and reinterpret the world around us. It is more than just a technical procedure. It is essential to our ability to communicate, learn, and express ourselves. The fundamental ideas of creative reuse have been a part of human culture for centuries, even though the digital revolution has surely increased the size and scope of remixing. To comprehend the dynamics of modern culture and the future of creativity, one must grasp the idea of remix in its widest sense.

➢ Examining the Folklore, Literature, and Art Historical Foundations of Remixing Outside of Digital Technology

The practice of remixing, or taking preexisting elements and combining them in new ways, has a long and rich history that predates the invention of computers and the internet, even though the term *"remix"* is frequently linked to digital culture and the ease with which digital media can be altered and shared. By following these historical origins, it becomes clear that remixing is an essential component of human creativity and cultural transmission rather than a relatively new phenomenon. Examples from literature, art, and folklore are examined to show how persistent this practice is.

The oral tradition and folklore:

Oral tradition and folklore may contain the oldest examples of remixing. Through oral tradition, stories, myths, legends, and songs were transmitted from one generation to the next, continuously being recounted, modified, and reinterpreted. Every performer or storyteller would add their own subtleties, taking into account the audience's expectations, their own experiences, and the particular cultural context. This ongoing process of adaptation and variation is a blatant illustration of remixing.

Think about the enormous collection of folktales from many cultures. Each version is distinct, reflecting the particular cultural and historical context in which it was told, even though many have similar motifs, characters, and plot structures. For instance, there are many different versions of the Cinderella story in the world, each with a unique cultural flair. The main plot of the story—a persecuted young woman who finds happiness through magical intervention—remains the same, but there are significant differences in the setting, the names of the characters, and the particular magical elements. An obvious example of remixing in oral tradition is this process of modifying and reinterpreting preexisting narratives.

In a similar vein, as folk songs and ballads were transmitted from one generation to the next, they were continually modified and reinterpreted. In order to reflect the evolving tastes and experiences of the communities that performed them, new verses would be added, lyrics would be changed, and melodies would be modified. This dynamic adaptation process demonstrated the ability of remixing to preserve cultural traditions by ensuring that these songs remained meaningful and relevant to each new generation.

Literature and the Tradition of Writing:

The history of literature is also steeped in the practice of remixing. In order to create new stories, writers have long taken inspiration from previously published works, utilizing characters, plot points, and stylistic devices. One important component of remix culture is the practice of intertextuality, or the relationship between texts.

Several instances of remixing can be found in classical literature. Existing myths and legends were reinterpreted for the stage by Greek playwrights such as Euripides and Sophocles in order to examine current social and political issues. Homer was a major source of inspiration for Roman poets such as Virgil, who adapted and reinterpreted the epic stories of the Odyssey and the Iliad in his own epic poem, the Aeneid. These adaptations were imaginative reinterpretations that took into account the shifting historical and cultural context rather than being simple copies.

Shakespeare was a master remixer and perhaps the most influential author in English. He created his own original dramatic works by heavily referencing pre-existing sources, such as historical chronicles, Italian novellas, and classical plays. For instance, Romeo and Juliet is inspired by Italian literature, while Hamlet is based on an older Scandinavian legend. Shakespeare's brilliance is found in his ability to turn preexisting stories into classic pieces of art as well as in his ability to develop likable characters and dramatic scenarios.

Examples of more recent literature include Tom Stoppard's Rosencrantz and Guildenstern Are Dead, a play that retells Hamlet's events from the viewpoint of two minor characters, and Jean Rhys's Wide Sargasso Sea, a postcolonial reimagining of Charlotte Brontë's Jane Eyre. These pieces show how remixing can be used to explore intricate themes and ideas and provide fresh viewpoints on preexisting narratives.

Visual Culture and Art:

The history of art and visual culture also demonstrates the practice of remixing. In order to produce new works of art, artists have long taken inspiration from earlier works, utilizing stylistic devices, compositional strategies, and subject matter.

For instance, artists heavily remixed works of art during the Renaissance, taking inspiration from classical Greek and Roman art. While painters like Raphael and Leonardo da Vinci used classical motifs and compositional principles in their own works, sculptors like Michelangelo and Donatello studied and reinterpreted classical sculptures. In the visual arts, remixing is exemplified by this process of taking inspiration from the past and reinterpreting it in a fresh way.

A number of artistic movements that openly supported the practice of remixing emerged in the 20th century. Collage, which was popularized by artists like Picasso and Braque, was the process of creating new artworks by fusing disparate materials like found objects, fabric scraps, and newspaper clippings. One of the main components of remix culture is the method of contrasting various objects and visuals to produce new meaning.

Through methods like photomontage and assemblage, Dadaism and Surrealism further investigated the potential of remixing, fusing disparate objects and images to produce surreal and frequently unnerving compositions. These movements embraced the idea that art could be produced by reusing and recontextualizing preexisting materials, challenging conventional ideas of originality and authorship.

Examining the origins of remixing shows that it is an essential component of human creativity and cultural transmission rather than a relatively new phenomenon. Remixing has been a consistent practice throughout history, ranging from the adaptation of folk tales to the reworking of classical literature and the repurposing of artistic styles. The fundamental ideas of creative reuse have been a part of human culture for centuries, even though digital technologies have surely increased the size and scope of remixing. It is essential to comprehend these historical foundations in order to comprehend the dynamics of modern remix culture and its position within the larger framework of human creativity.

➤ **Setting the stage for the central question: Is everything a remix?**

The main focus of this investigation into remix culture is the question, *"Is everything a remix?"* It's a thought-provoking query that questions accepted ideas about creativity, originality, and authorship. A straightforward *"yes"* or *"no"* response may seem alluring, but the truth is much more intricate and subtle. Establishing a clear understanding of what *"remix"* means in a broad cultural context, recognizing the historical precedents of remixing, and defining the main areas of inquiry that will be investigated are all necessary to set the stage for this central question.

As was previously mentioned, a remix is the process of combining or changing preexisting elements—such as sounds, images, texts, ideas, or cultural practices—to produce something new. Remix culture is characterized by this process of reusing and recontextualizing. Transforming and reinterpreting, adding new levels of meaning, and developing new forms of expression are more important than merely copying or reproducing. This definition, which separates remixing from simple plagiarism or duplication, is essential for posting the main query.

Remixing is not a new phenomenon; rather, it is a basic component of human creativity, as shown by its historical precedents in literature, art, and folklore. Remixing has been a consistent practice throughout history, ranging from the adaptation of folk tales to the reworking of classical literature and the repurposing of artistic styles. Understanding the larger cultural context in which the question *"Is everything a remix?"* is posed requires an awareness of these historical foundations. It proves that human culture has a strong inclination to appropriate, modify, and change preexisting works.

However, there is no denying that the size and reach of remixing have increased with the introduction of digital technologies. Remixing has become a common cultural practice, and the process of creating content has become more accessible due to the ease with which digital content can be copied, altered, and shared. The main question is given a new dimension by this digital context, which brings up concerns about intellectual property, copyright, and how technology affects creative processes.

"Is everything a remix?" is more than just a semantic query. It poses important queries regarding what originality is. What does it mean to be *"original"* if all creative works are influenced by earlier works and originality is frequently a question of degree rather than complete invention? Is all creativity a kind of remixing, or is there no such thing as true originality?

The idea of authorship is also touched upon in this investigation. The conventional idea of the lone author as the only creator of a work is called into question in a remix culture, where works are frequently produced through collaboration and the reuse of preexisting materials. Since the remixer is not only replicating but also reinterpreting and changing preexisting works while contributing their own creative touch, their role becomes vital. Given how simple it is to copy and distribute content in the digital age, this calls into question ownership and intellectual property.

In addition, the query, **"Is everything a remix?"** makes us think about how context shapes meaning. When preexisting elements are combined in a new context, new meanings and interpretations are produced. A remixed work is more than just the sum of its parts. Depending on the context in which it is used, the same element can have multiple meanings. This emphasizes how crucial it is to comprehend the historical and cultural setting in which a remix is produced and listened to.

In order to answer the main question, several important fields of study will be investigated:

Remixing is a spectrum that includes everything from subtle references and influences to overt sampling and adaptation. It is essential to comprehend this spectrum in order to differentiate between various remixing styles and assess their creative value.

The part transformation plays: The process of transformation is a crucial component of remixing. A remix entails changing, reinterpreting, and giving previously existing elements new meaning; a simple copy is not a remix. One important determinant of a remix's uniqueness and creative worth is the extent of transformation.

The effects of technology Remix culture has been greatly influenced by digital technologies, which have made it simpler than ever to produce and distribute remixed content. To comprehend the modern forms of remixing, it is imperative to investigate the role of technology.

The ethical and legal ramifications: Remixing brings up significant issues with fair use, intellectual property, and copyright. Navigating the intricacies of remix culture require a close examination of these ethical and legal aspects.

Remixing is not only a creative activity; it is also a cultural and social phenomenon that has a big impact on how we produce, consume, and distribute culture. To completely understand the significance of the question, *"Is everything a remix?"* one must be aware of this wider impact. By examining these fields of study, this work seeks to answer the main question in a thorough and perceptive manner while offering a nuanced understanding of remix culture. The intention is to encourage critical thinking and debate regarding the nature of creativity, originality, and authorship in the digital age rather than to offer a conclusive response. An in-depth investigation of the dynamic and constantly changing terrain of modern culture begins with the query, *"Is everything a remix?"*

➤ **Overview of the book's structure and key arguments.**

This book, *"The Remix Generation: Is Everything a Remix?"* delves deeply into the phenomenon of remix culture, which has influenced modern creativity and cultural production. This investigation's main question, *"Is everything a remix?"* provides a prism through which to view the origins, current applications, and potential future ramifications of remixing. This synopsis will give a road map for the future by outlining the book's organization and main points.

The book is divided into ten chapters, each of which focuses on a different aspect of remix culture and builds on the one before it to provide a coherent and thorough understanding. Both chronologically and thematically, the story advances from historical precedents to modern practices before speculating about potential future developments.

Overview: The Message in the Remix: The foundation for the entire book is laid out in this introductory chapter. The term *"remix"* is defined in a broad cultural context that goes beyond digital manipulation to include a variety of creative re-use techniques, such as pastiche, adaptation, appropriation, and sampling. This chapter makes the case that the act of remixing itself becomes the main message, recontextualizing the original elements and producing new interpretations, drawing inspiration from Marshall McLuhan's theory that *"the medium is the message."* Additionally, it explores the origins of remixing, showing that it is an essential component of human creativity rather than a relatively new phenomenon. Lastly, it introduces the main query, *"Is everything a remix?"* and lists the main research topics that will be covered.

Chapter 1: Historical Reverberations: Pre-Digital Remixing The historical precedents of remixing prior to the development of digital technology are explored in this chapter. It looks at instances from oral tradition and folklore, where songs and stories were continuously modified and reinterpreted as they were transmitted from one generation to the next. It also looks at examples of remixing in art, like the Renaissance's reworking of classical styles, and in literature, like Shakespeare's adaptations of pre-existing stories. By proving that the desire to appropriate, modify, and alter preexisting works is a fundamental aspect of human culture, this chapter establishes the continuity of remixing as a human creative practice.

Chapter 2: Digital Revolution: Transformational Tools: The significant influence of digital technologies on remixing is the main topic of this chapter. It looks at how remixing has become a common cultural practice and how the ease with which digital content can be copied, altered, and shared has democratized the creative process. It investigates how software tools for text processing, image manipulation, and audio and video editing can reduce the technical barriers to entry. Additionally, it talks about how the internet is a huge collection of easily accessible content that is open to sampling and repurposing. This chapter focuses on how remixing has expanded in size and scope due to digital technology, opening up new avenues for artistic expression.

Chapter 3: The Remix Dilemma: Copyright and Creativity The complicated ethical and legal ramifications of remixing are covered in this chapter, with special attention to copyright and intellectual property. It looks at the conflict between promoting creativity and defending the rights of creators. It discusses how fair use and transformative use relate to remixed works and examines the controversy surrounding these terms. It also talks about alternative licensing models like Creative Commons and looks at case studies of copyright disputes involving remixed content. In the context of remix culture, this chapter negotiates the frequently tense nexus of creativity, technology, and law.

Chapter 4: Remixed Music: From Mashups to Sampling The function of remixing in music is the particular subject of this chapter. From the earliest types of sampling to the emergence of mashups and other modern techniques, it examines the development and history of music remixing. It talks about famous remixes and their cultural impact, as well as how genres like hip-hop and electronic music have influenced remix culture. This chapter offers a thorough analysis of the ways in which remixing has changed the creation and consumption of music.

Chapter 5: Remixing Visual Culture: From Memes to Fan Art This chapter examines the function of remixing in visual culture, turning its attention to the visual world. It explores the ways in which participatory culture, such as fan art, fan fiction, and internet memes, facilitate the remixing of visual content. It also looks at how remixing is used in marketing, propaganda, and advertising. This chapter illustrates how ubiquitous remixing is in forming our visual environment.

Chapter 6: Narrative Remixed: Transmedia Storytelling, Retellings, and Adaptations This chapter explores the idea of narrative remixing in a variety of media, such as video games, television, movies, and books. It investigates how prequels, sequels, remakes, and adaptations can expand and reinterpret already-existing stories. The rise of transmedia storytelling, which depends on repurposing story components on various platforms, is also covered. This chapter demonstrates how remixing has emerged as a key technique in modern narrative.

Chapter 7: Identity Remixed: Digital Age Self-Presentation: The way people remix their identities in the digital age is examined in this chapter. It explores how people create and present themselves online using avatars, profiles, and other forms of self-representation, as well as how social media shapes online identities. Additionally, it examines the idea of ***"digital selves"*** and how they relate to actual identities, emphasizing how identity is flexible and changeable in virtual environments.

Chapter 8: The Morality of Remixing: Ownership, Authorship, and Appropriation This chapter explores the intricacies of appropriation, authorship, and ownership as it digs deeper into the moral implications of remixing. It explores the ethical issues surrounding borrowing from preexisting works and looks at the difference between appropriation and inspiration. In a remix culture, where works are frequently produced through collaboration and reuse, it also reexamines the issue of authorship. This chapter offers a thoughtful analysis of the moral dilemmas and possibilities that remixing presents.

Chapter 9: Remixing's Future: AI, Algorithms, and Other Developments This chapter examines the possible effects of cutting-edge technologies like algorithms and artificial intelligence on the future of remixing. In discussing the emergence of generative AI and its effects on creative production, it poses queries regarding the future of intellectual property and copyright in an era of AI-generated content. In light of the changing dynamic between humans and machines in creative processes, it also makes predictions about potential future trends in remix culture.

Is everything a remix? A More Complex Viewpoint: The book's main query, *"Is everything a remix?"* is revisited in this final chapter, which provides a nuanced viewpoint that recognizes the intricacies and paradoxes of remix culture. It brings the many strands of the discussion together and summarizes the main points and conclusions of the earlier chapters. The act of remixing entails not only copying but also changing and reinterpreting, adding new meaning and value, even though all creative works are influenced by earlier works and originality is frequently a matter of degree.

The book seeks to offer a thorough and perceptive grasp of remix culture, including its historical foundations, current expressions, and potential future developments through this methodical investigation. It makes the case that remixing is not merely a technical procedure but rather a basic component of human creativity and cultural transmission, influencing the way we produce, consume, and perceive the world.

Chapter 1:

Echoes of the Past: Pre-Digital Remixing

The word *"remix"* is frequently connected to the digital era, evoking visions of edited videos, repurposed online content, and sampled music. But even before the invention of digital technology, the basic ideas of remixing—taking preexisting elements and combining them in novel ways—had been a catalyst for human creativity for centuries. Remixing is not a new phenomenon; rather, it is a deeply embedded part of human culture, as evidenced by the rich history of creative re-use across disciplines found in pre-digital forms.

Oral Tradition and Narrative's Flexibility:

Oral tradition is one of the oldest and most widespread types of pre-digital remixing. Stories, myths, legends, and songs were passed down orally from one generation to the next prior to the widespread use of writing. There was inevitably some remixing involved in this oral transmission process. As a result of their unique style, cultural background, and audience's particular requirements, every storyteller, singer, or performer would unavoidably add their own subtleties, interpretations, and embellishments to the content.

Because of the oral tradition's narrative fluidity, stories were continually being rewritten and reinterpreted. Depending on the social setting, moral lessons may be emphasized or minimized, characters may be given new motivations, and plotlines may be changed to reflect current events. Remixing is evident in this dynamic process of adaptation and reinterpretation. Think of the many cultural variations of classic stories like Little Red Riding Hood or Cinderella. The remixing effect of oral transmission is demonstrated by the fact that, although the essential narrative elements are frequently still identifiable, the specific details, cultural settings and moral lessons can differ greatly.

Variations in Music and the Art of Metamorphosis:

Another excellent example of pre-digital remixing is found in music. There are numerous instances of composers appropriating, modifying, and transforming preexisting musical material, especially in the classical music tradition. A mainstay of classical composition, the variation form expressly entails taking a theme (a melody or harmonic progression) and putting it through a number of changes. These modifications could create new and unique versions of the original material by changing the melody, harmony, rhythm, tempo, or instrumentation.

The variation form was mastered by composers such as Ludwig van Beethoven, Wolfgang Amadeus Mozart, and Johann Sebastian Bach. For example, Bach's Goldberg Variations begins with a straightforward aria and then features thirty variations that each explore various musical styles and techniques. A rather straightforward waltz by Anton Diabelli is transformed into a monumental piece of music with great depth and complexity by Beethoven's Diabelli Variations. These illustrations show how composers can uncover new dimensions and expressive possibilities in preexisting musical material by utilizing the variation form.

In addition to using the variation form, composers also adapted and arranged existing works, reworking them for various ensembles or instruments. For instance, Bach arranged and transsscribed many of Vivaldi's concertos for organ and harpsichord. In addition to making Vivaldi's music more widely available, these adaptations gave Bach the chance to examine and reinterpret the Italian composer's style using his own distinctive musical perspective.

Reimagining narratives and literary adaptations:

There are many examples of pre-digital remixing in literature as well. For a very long time, authors have adapted and reimagined characters, plots, and themes from previous works in order to find inspiration. A crucial component of literary remixing is the practice of intertextuality, or the relationship between texts.

For the Athenian stage, Greek playwrights such as Sophocles and Euripides reinterpreted pre-existing myths and legends to examine current social and political issues. Shakespeare, who was a master of adaptation, transformed classical plays, Italian novellas, and historical chronicles into timeless dramatic masterpieces. For instance, Romeo and Juliet is inspired by Italian mythology, while Hamlet is based on an earlier Scandinavian legend.

This tradition of retelling and adaptation was carried on by later literary movements like

Victorianism and Romanticism. To produce a fresh and significant work of horror and science fiction, authors such as Mary Shelley drew on pre-existing Gothic clichés and philosophical concepts in Frankenstein. These instances show how writers can converse with the past through literary adaptation, rewriting classic stories for fresh audiences, and investigating novel concepts and themes.

The Conversation with the Past and Artistic Appropriation:

In the visual arts, artistic appropriation—the practice of artists taking and reinterpreting pre-existing works or styles—was the precursor to digital remixing. Classical Greek and Roman art served as a source of inspiration for Renaissance artists, who adopted its themes, methods, and principles into their own creations. The Renaissance's artistic style was greatly influenced by this rediscovery and reinterpretation of classical art.

Neoclassicism and Romanticism were two later artistic movements that carried on this tradition of interacting with the past. While Romantic artists frequently turned to medieval and folk traditions, Neoclassical artists were influenced by classical art and architecture. These illustrations show how artists can converse with the past through artistic appropriation, reinterpreting established styles and traditions in fresh and significant ways.

These examples from literature, art, music, and oral tradition show that remixing is a basic component of human creativity that has existed for centuries rather than being a product of the digital age. Remixing before the advent of digital technology was essential for influencing culture, spreading knowledge, and encouraging creative expression. We can better appreciate the relevance of remixing in modern culture and acknowledge its enduring power as a creative force by comprehending these historical foundations.

1.1 Exploring examples of remixing in pre-digital eras:

The idea of remixing has roots in pre-digital history and is frequently connected to contemporary digital technology. Remixing existed in many forms prior to the invention of computers and the internet, influencing communication, art, and culture.

Storytelling and Oral Tradition

Oral tradition and storytelling are among the oldest examples of remixing. Stories, myths, and legends were transmitted orally from generation to generation prior to the development of writing. Every storyteller would give the story a different twist by fusing current affairs, cultural quirks, and personal experiences. Numerous versions of the same story, each a remix of the original, were produced as a result of this process of retelling and reinterpretation.

Adaptations and Variations in Music

Another excellent example of pre-digital remixing is found in music. Throughout history, composers have created new works by incorporating melodies, harmonies, and rhythms from preexisting pieces. Numerous classical works employ this technique, which is called musical variation. The ***"Goldberg Variations"*** by Johann Sebastian Bach, for example, are a collection of thirty variations on a single theme. Every variation demonstrates the composer's talent and inventiveness by taking the original melody and turning it into a brand-new, original composition.

Literary Retellings and Adaptations

Examples of pre-digital remixing abound in literature. Authors have long used previously published works as a source of inspiration, reimagining themes, characters, and plots in fresh and creative ways. Myths and legends were adapted for the stage by Greek playwrights like Euripides and Sophocles, who added modern social and political commentary. William Shakespeare is renowned for taking characters and plots from other works and turning them into classics like ***"Hamlet"*** and ***"Romeo and Juliet."***

Reinterpretation and artisticappropriation

Pre-digital remixing also flourished in the art world. Throughout history, artists have appropriated and reinterpreted preexisting works to produce new works that expand on them. For instance, there was a resurgence of interest in classical Greek and Roman art during the Renaissance. Classical sculptures and paintings were studied and reinterpreted by Renaissance artists like Michelangelo and Raphael, who added their own distinct styles and viewpoints. Through ongoing conversations with the past, artists have perpetuated this process of artistic appropriation and reinterpretation throughout history.

Intercultural Communication and Syncretism

Pre-digital remixing also happened as a result of syncretism and cultural interchange. Ideas, traditions, and customs were shared as cultures came together and interacted. As a result of this process, various cultural components were frequently blended to create new hybrid forms. For example, the Silk Road, an antiquated system of trade routes that linked the East and West, made it easier for people to share products, concepts, and cultural customs. Various cultural elements, including religious beliefs, artistic styles, and culinary traditions, were remixed as a result of this exchange.

These illustrations show that remixing is a centuries-old practice rather than a recent occurrence. Remixing before the digital age has been essential to the development of communication, art, and culture. We can better appreciate remixing's importance in the digital age if we are aware of its historical foundations.

1.2 Variations and Adaptations of Classical Music: A Tradition Before Digital Remix

The idea of remixing has a rich pre-digital history in the classical music tradition of adaptations and variations, despite being frequently linked to modern digital culture. These techniques, which have a long history in Western music, show a deep comprehension of how to create fresh and captivating works from preexisting musical material. A type of creative re-use is represented by variations and adaptations, in which a composer uses a variety of techniques to reinterpret an existing melody, harmonic progression, or even an entire composition, offering new insights into the source material. The subtleties of these practices will be examined in this essay, along with their historical significance and how they exemplify the spirit of remixing in a pre-digital setting.

The Variation Form: Revealing Potential That Was Hidden

A fundamental component of classical music, the variation form entails introducing a theme (a melody or harmonic progression) and then transforming it in a number of ways.

These changes, referred to as variations, can change a number of musical components, such as:

Melody: The original melody may be transposed, inverted, embellished, or broken up.
Harmony: You can change the harmonic rhythm or add new chords to the underlying harmonies.
Rhythm: Various note values, syncopation, or tempo adjustments can be used to alter the rhythmic structure.
Texture: Adding or removing voices, adjusting the instrumentation, or changing the music's density can all change the texture.
Tempo and Meter: The theme can have a different personality by varying the tempo and meter.

Variations aim to explore the theme's hidden potential, exposing new dimensions and expressive possibilities rather than merely repeating it in a different way. Every variation presents a distinct viewpoint on the source material, evoking a feeling of both familiarity and originality.

Examples of Variations in History:

The variation form has been used by many composers throughout history to produce some of the most enduring pieces in the classical repertoire. Among the noteworthy instances are:

The Goldberg Variations (BWV 988) by Johann Sebastian Bach is a monumental work that consists of 30 variations, each of which explores a different musical style and technique, and a theme (an aria). Bach's mastery of counterpoint and harmonic inventiveness are demonstrated by the variations' methodical progression, which also conveys a sense of architectural grandeur.

The Twelve Variations on *"Ah vous dirai-je, Maman"* by Wolfgang Amadeus Mozart (K. 265): Mozart's ability to produce sophisticated and endearing variations on a straightforward melody is demonstrated in this collection of variations on the French folk tune *"Ah vous dirai-je, Maman"* (better known as *"Twinkle Twinkle Little Star")*.

The Diabelli Variations by Ludwig van Beethoven (Op. 120): There are 33 variations on a waltz by Anton Diabelli in this enormous piece. Beethoven's variations cover a wide spectrum of musical genres and moods, from lighthearted and playful to somber and reflective.

Haydn's Variations on a Theme (Op. 56a) by Johannes Brahms: The theme of this orchestral piece is taken from a St. Anthony Chorale, which Brahms thought was composed by Joseph Haydn. The variations demonstrate Brahms' skill as an orchestral composer and his capacity to produce textures that are rich and expressive.

Changes: Reimagining Already-Existing Works

Another type of pre-digital remixing is adaptation, which entails reworking an existing piece for a new instrumentation or medium. Simple transcriptions to intricate arrangements that drastically change the original work are examples of this practice.

Adaptation Types:

Rewriting a piece for a different instrument or ensemble while maintaining as much of the original musical content as possible is known as a transcription. A violin sonata may be transcribed for cello, or a piano composition may be transcribed for orchestra.

Adapting a composition for a new medium or instrumentation while making more substantial modifications to the musical content is known as an arrangement. This could entail modifying the instrumentation, adding new harmonies, or changing the composition's structure.

Fantasias and paraphrases are adaptations in which a theme or melody from an already-existing work serves as the inspiration for a brand-new song. Unlike a straightforward arrangement, the original material is frequently developed and altered in a more creative and unrestricted manner.

Examples of Adaptations in the Past:

Bach's transcriptions and arrangements of Vivaldi concertos: Bach modified the Italian composer's style by transcribing and arranging a number of Vivaldi concertos for organ and piano.
Liszt's virtuoso piano transcriptions of Beethoven's symphonies: Franz Liszt made Beethoven's orchestral works more widely available by creating virtuosic piano transcriptions of his works.
Brahms's arrangements of Hungarian Dances: Brahms composed lively and well-liked pieces for piano four-hands based on a collection of Hungarian folk tunes.

The Classical Music Remixing Spirit:

By taking preexisting musical material and turning it into something new, both adaptations and variations embody the spirit of remixing. They show that being creative doesn't always mean creating something from the ground up; it can also mean reinterpreting and reimagining previously created works. These methods demonstrate how tradition and innovation interact dynamically in classical music, where composers are always interacting with the past while expanding the possibilities for musical expression.

Fascinating pre-digital examples of remixing can be found in the traditions of variations and adaptations in classical music. They exhibit a deep comprehension of how to use a variety of techniques to transform preexisting musical material, resulting in fresh interpretations of original works. These practices demonstrate the ability of remixing to enhance and broaden our cultural landscape while highlighting the persistent human impulse to borrow, adapt, and reinterpret.

1.3 Examining Retellings and Adaptations in Literature

For centuries, retelling and adapting stories has been a fundamental part of literary expression among artists. For a very long time, writers have been inspired by pre-existing stories, reworking characters, plots, and themes to produce new works that appeal to modern audiences. In addition to giving timeless stories new life, the process of literary adaptation and retelling makes it possible to investigate various viewpoints, cultural settings, and artistic movements.

Shakespeare's Adaptations: An Exquisite Example of Narration

William Shakespeare was a master of literary adaptation and is considered by many to be the best writer in the English language. He created timeless masterpieces by regularly appropriating plots and characters from pre-existing sources, such as historical chronicles, Italian novellas, and classical plays.

"Hamlet," a tragedy thought to be based on the story of Amleth, a Danish prince who exacts revenge for the death of his father, is one of Shakespeare's most well-known adaptations. Shakespeare's adaptation explores themes of retaliation, insanity, and death while probing the protagonist's innermost thoughts.

Another noteworthy example is the romantic tragedy *"Romeo and Juliet,"* which is based on a number of Italian sources, such as Arthur Brooke's poem *"The Tragical History of Romeus and Juliet."* Shakespeare's adaptation captures the passion and tragedy of young love, taking the story to new dramatic heights.

Additional Prominent Literary Adaptations

The practice of literary adaptation has been adopted by other authors besides Shakespeare. Throughout history, numerous other authors have given old tales new life by reimagining them.

Jean Rhys' *"Wide Sargasso Sea"*: The 1966 book is a feminist and postcolonial reaction to Charlotte Bront's "Jane Eyre." Through Rhys' reimagining of the tale of Antoinette Cosway, the "madwoman in the attic," a previously marginalized and silenced character is given a voice.

Margaret Atwood's 2005 novella *"The Penelopiad"* retells Homer's *"Odyssey"* from the viewpoint of Odysseus's wife, Penelope. By examining themes of female agency and domesticity, Atwood's adaptation provides novel and perceptive interpretation of the epic poem.

Frank Herbert's 1965 science fiction book *"Dune"* is regarded as a genre classic. Herbert creates a sophisticated and thought-provoking story by drawing inspiration from a variety of sources, such as historical occurrences, religious customs, and environmental issues.

The Advantages of Adapting Literature

Both authors and readers can benefit from literary adaptation in a number of ways. It gives writers a wealth of ideas and enables them to retell well-known tales in novel ways. It gives readers a new and exciting way to interact with classic stories.

Additionally, adaptation can aid in bridging linguistic and cultural divides, increasing the accessibility of classic works for audiences in the modern era. Authors can make sure that these tales remain relevant to readers of all ages by modernizing the language, settings, and themes.

The literary landscape has been significantly shaped by literary retelling and adaptation. Authors honor the past while simultaneously producing new works that speak to the present by reimagining old tales. Literature is a dynamic and ever-evolving art form because of this constant conversation between the past and present.

1.4 The Development of Folk Music Through Oral Tradition

Folk music is a type of music that has strong roots in the customs and culture of a specific group of people or area. It is frequently distinguished by its use of traditional instruments, catchy rhythms, and straightforward melodies. Additionally, folk music is usually transmitted orally, which means that it is learned and performed by ear rather than using written notation.

The development of folk music over time has been significantly influenced by this oral tradition. Songs are frequently modified and adapted as they are passed down from one generation to the next in order to reflect the shifting times and the individual experiences of the singers. Folk music's distinct personality and vitality come from this process of adaptation and change.

Variation is one of the most significant ways that folk music has changed over time through oral tradition. Small alterations will inevitably happen over time when a song is transmitted orally. These alterations could be purposeful, like a singer adding their own unique touch to a song, or they could be inadvertent, like a singer forgetting a word or phrase. These minor adjustments can add up over time to produce notable variations in a song's melody, lyrics, or rhythm.

The process of borrowing is another significant way that oral tradition has shaped folk music. The melodies, lyrics, and rhythmic elements of other songs or musical traditions are frequently appropriated by folk musicians. This borrowing process can result in the adaptation of existing songs to a new cultural context or in the creation of new songs based on preexisting material.

Folk music has also been preserved in part through the oral tradition. Folk music is regarded as an essential component of the cultural heritage of the community in many cultures. Communities can guarantee the perpetuation of their music by transferring songs orally.

The development of folk music in the modern era has been significantly influenced by the internet. Folk musicians now have an easier time reaching a worldwide audience thanks to the internet. Additionally, it has made it simpler for people to discover and enjoy folk music from other cultures.

Folk music is now more accessible and varied than ever before, thanks to the internet. Folk musicians are using the internet to connect with one another and share their music with the world, and there are now folk music communities all over the world.

The oral tradition-based development of folk music is a continuous process. Folk music will continue to develop and change as long as there are people who are enthusiastic about it.

Here are some particular instances of how oral tradition has shaped folk music:

The development of the ballad: A folk song that narrates a story is called a ballad. Originally transmitted orally, ballads frequently underwent substantial changes over time. Numerous renditions of the ballad *"The Twa Corbies"* exist, each with its own distinct melody, lyrics, and narrative.

The blues' development The blues is a type of African American folk music that has its roots in the American South. Call-and-response vocals, improvisational melodies, and the use of blue notes are characteristics of the blues. Over the years, the blues has undergone significant change and influenced many other musical genres, such as jazz, rock, and country.

Folk music's development in the digital era: Folk musicians now have an easier time reaching a worldwide audience thanks to the internet. As a result, new folk music subgenres like indie folk and folk-punk have emerged. People can now more easily learn about and enjoy folk music from other cultures thanks to the internet.

The way folk music has developed through oral tradition is evidence of how creative people can be. Communities can guarantee the perpetuation of their music by transferring songs from one generation to the next. Folk musicians now find it simpler to communicate with one another and spread their music globally thanks to the internet. Folk music has become more accessible and varied as a result.

I would like to add the following to the previously mentioned:

Folk music has developed in ways other than oral tradition. Pop, world, and classical music are just a few of the musical genres that have influenced folk music.
Folk music is constantly changing and evolving. Folk music will continue to develop and change as long as there are people who are enthusiastic about it.
The tradition of folk music is alive and well. The people who play and sing it are continuously creating and re-creating it.
I hope this essay has given you a better understanding of how oral tradition has shaped folk music.

1.5 The Impact of Previous Artistic Movements on Later Ones

Similar to pond ripples, artistic movements produce waves of influence that cut across time and cultural boundaries. Every movement has a lasting impact on the art world and shapes the course of later artistic expression because it was born out of a distinct set of social, political, and technological circumstances. This essay will look at how artists borrow, modify, and defy established styles to produce fresh and inventive works of art, demonstrating the significant impact of earlier artistic movements on those that came after.

The Renaissance and Classicism's Rebirth

There was a resurgence of interest in the classical art of ancient Greece and Rome during the Renaissance, a time of great artistic and cultural flourishing in Europe. Renaissance artists like Michelangelo, Raphael, and Leonardo da Vinci studied and imitated classical ideals, proportions, and forms, then incorporated them into their own creations. Neoclassicism and academic art were two later artistic movements that were significantly influenced by this resurgence of classicism.

Baroque and the Increasing Intensity of Emotion

Following the Renaissance, the Baroque era was distinguished by a dramatic and sentimental aesthetic. By employing dramatic lighting, dynamic compositions, and expressive figures, Baroque artists like Caravaggio, Bernini, and Rembrandt aimed to arouse strong emotions in their audience. Later movements like Romanticism and Expressionism were influenced by the Baroque emphasis on dramatic expression and emotional intensity.

The Acceptance of Individualism and Romanticism

The late 18th-century Romantic movement placed a strong emphasis on emotion, individualism, and the force of nature. Imagination, intuition, and the sublime were embraced by romantic artists like Caspar David Friedrich, William Blake, and J. M. W. Turner, who rejected Neoclassicism's order and 理⁻. Later movements like Impressionism and Symbolism were made possible by the Romantic movement's emphasis on personal expression and emotional intensity.

Impressionism and Modern Art's Inception

With its emphasis on preserving the ephemeral impressions of color and light, the Impressionist movement, which first appeared in the late 19th century, completely changed the art world. Impressionists like Claude Monet, Pierre-Auguste Renoir, and Edgar Degas forsake conventional representational methods in favor of expressive brushwork and vivid hues to portray the sensory experience of their surroundings. Modern art developed as a result of Impressionism's rejection of conventional artistic conventions and emphasis on subjective perception.

20th Century Developments and the Spread of "-isms"

A plethora of artistic movements, each with its own distinct style and philosophy, emerged during the 20th century. Artists challenged conventional ideas of art and beauty by experimenting with new forms of representation, from Fauvism and Expressionism to Cubism, Surrealism, and Abstract Expressionism. Despite having different approaches and styles, these movements had one thing in common: a desire to reject the past and invent something fresh.

The Postmodern Era and the Dissolution of Distinctions

The distinctions between various artistic movements and styles are becoming less clear in the postmodern era, which started in the late 20th century. Postmodern artists frequently find inspiration in a variety of places, such as mass media, popular culture, and earlier artistic movements. New and hybrid forms of art have emerged as a result of this eclectic approach, reflecting the modern world's growing interconnectedness and globalization.

Art history is dynamic and interconnected, as evidenced by the impact of earlier artistic movements on later ones. In order to produce fresh and inventive forms of expression, artists are always interacting with the past, appropriating, modifying, and defying conventional styles. Art will always be a dynamic and ever-evolving representation of the human condition, thanks to this continuous process of artistic development.

1.6 Establishing the continuity of remixing as a human creative practice.

The idea of remixing, which is frequently linked to the digital era and the ease with which media can be altered, is not a recent development. With roots in ancient times, it is a practice that is profoundly embedded in human creativity. Analyzing different pre-digital remixing techniques demonstrates an ongoing pattern of imaginative reuse, modification, and metamorphosis that highlights the innate human desire to expand on preexisting concepts and creations.

Oral Traditions: The First Platform for Remixing

Oral traditions were the main way that knowledge, stories, and cultural values were passed down long before writing was invented. Because each storyteller acted as a remixer, modifying the narrative to fit their audience, context, and personal style, these traditions were by their very nature dynamic and fluid. Stories were dynamic, ever-evolving works of art that were continually being rewritten and reinterpreted with each new telling.

Narratives naturally varied as a result of this oral transmission process. Depending on the social setting, moral lessons may be emphasized or minimized, characters may be given new motivations, and plotlines may be changed to reflect current events. This intrinsic diversity shows that remixing is an essential part of human communication and cultural transmission rather than just a byproduct of digital technology.

Musical Variations: Melodies That Change Over Time

Another powerful example of pre-digital remixing is found in music. There are numerous instances of composers appropriating, modifying, and transforming preexisting musical material, especially in classical music tradition. A mainstay of classical composition, the variation form expressly entails taking a theme (a melody or harmonic progression) and putting it through a number of changes. These modifications could create new and unique versions of the original material by changing the melody, harmony, rhythm, tempo, or instrumentation.

The variation form was mastered by composers such as Ludwig van Beethoven, Wolfgang Amadeus Mozart, and Johann Sebastian Bach. For example, Bach's Goldberg Variations begins with a straightforward aria and then features thirty variations that each explore various musical styles and techniques. A rather straightforward waltz by Anton Diabelli is transformed into a monumental piece of music with great depth and complexity by Beethoven's Diabelli Variations. These illustrations show how composers can uncover new dimensions and expressive possibilities in preexisting musical material by utilizing the variation form.

Literary Adaptations: Retelling Stories for Different audiences

There are many examples of pre-digital remixing in literature as well. For a very long time, authors have adapted and reimagined characters, plots, and themes from previous works in order to find inspiration. A crucial component of literary remixing is the practice of intertextuality, or the relationship between texts.

For the Athenian stage, Greek playwrights such as Sophocles and Euripides reinterpreted pre-existing myths and legends to examine current social and political issues. Shakespeare, who was a master of adaptation, transformed classical plays, Italian novellas, and historical chronicles into timeless dramatic masterpieces. For instance, Romeo and Juliet is inspired by Italian mythology, while Hamlet is based on an earlier Scandinavian legend.

This tradition of retelling and adaptation was carried on by later literary movements like

Victorianism and Romanticism. To produce a fresh and significant work of horror and science fiction, authors such as Mary Shelley drew on pre-existing Gothic clichés and philosophical concepts in Frankenstein. These instances show how writers can converse with the past through literary adaptation, rewriting classic stories for fresh audiences, and investigating novel concepts and themes.

A Conversation Across Centuries on Artistic Appropriation

In the visual arts, artistic appropriation—the practice of artists taking and reinterpreting pre-existing works or styles—was the precursor to digital remixing. Classical Greek and Roman art served as a source of inspiration for Renaissance artists, who adopted its themes, methods, and principles into their own creations. The Renaissance's artistic style was greatly influenced by this rediscovery and reinterpretation of classical art.

Neoclassicism and Romanticism were two later artistic movements that carried on this tradition of interacting with the past. While Romantic artists frequently turned to medieval and folk traditions, Neoclassical artists were influenced by classical art and architecture. These illustrations show how artists can converse with the past through artistic appropriation, reinterpreting established styles and traditions in fresh and significant ways.

The Basic Human Impulse of Remixing

These examples from literature, art, music, and oral tradition show that remixing is a basic component of human creativity that has existed for centuries rather than being a product of the digital age. Remixing before the advent of digital technology was essential for influencing culture, spreading knowledge, and encouraging creative expression. We can better appreciate the relevance of remixing in modern culture and acknowledge its enduring power as a creative force by comprehending these historical foundations.

Chapter 2:

The Digital Revolution: Tools of Transformation

Remixing has seen significant change as a result of the digital revolution, which was characterized by the introduction of computers, the internet, and digital media. Although creative reuse was a practice long before the digital age, a new era of creative expression has been ushered in by the tools and technologies of the digital revolution, which have increased its scale, scope, and accessibility. This essay will examine how these digital tools have developed into potent transformational tools that allow for new kinds of remixing in a variety of media.

The Development of Digital Manipulation and Sampling

The emergence of digital sampling is one of the most important effects of the digital revolution on remix culture. Sampling is the process of incorporating a portion of an existing recording—a spoken word, a musical phrase, or a sound—into a new work of art. Prior to digital technology, sampling was a time-consuming and costly procedure that frequently called for specialized tools and technical know-how. But the process became more accessible with the introduction of digital samplers and computer software, making it simple for anybody with a computer to sample and work with audio.

Music has been greatly impacted by this ease of sampling, especially in dance, electronic, and hip-hop genres. In order to create fresh and inventive musical compositions, artists started sampling everything from vintage funk and soul records to dialogue and sound effects from movies. Sampling developed into a potent technique for rearranging preexisting sounds to produce fresh juxtapositions and meanings.

Digital tools have transformed image and video manipulation in addition to audio. The ease with which digital images and videos can now be edited, altered, and combined thanks to programs like Adobe Photoshop and After Effects has created new opportunities for visual remixing. In order to turn preexisting visual content into fresh and frequently surprising works, artists and creators started making photomontages, video mashups, and other types of visual remix.

The Internet as a Platform for Remixing:

With its extensive computer network and ability to share information quickly, the internet has emerged as a key platform for remix culture. Accessing, sharing, and disseminating digital content has never been simpler thanks to the internet, which has also produced a global library of easily accessible content for remixing.

Numerous examples of remixed music, videos, and other digital content can be found on websites like YouTube, SoundCloud, and Vimeo, which have developed into centers for remix culture. These platforms have also made it easier for online communities devoted to remixing to emerge, where artists can exchange their work, work together, and discuss remix culture.

Additionally, new remixing techniques that were not feasible prior to the digital era have been made possible by the internet. Internet memes, for instance, are a common form of online communication and cultural expression that frequently entail the modification and reinterpretation of preexisting images or phrases. As they are shared and reinterpreted by various users, these memes change and evolve as they quickly spread throughout the internet.

The democratization of artistic instruments

The democratization of creative tools is one of the biggest effects of the digital revolution on remix culture. Prior to the digital era, only people with expensive equipment or specialized training frequently had access to professional-grade creative tools. However, these tools are now available to a much larger audience thanks to the development of reasonably priced computers and intuitive software.

Now that software for image manipulation, graphic design, and audio and video editing is widely accessible and reasonably priced, anyone can make and distribute their own remixed content. With more people than ever before able to engage in remix culture, the democratization of creative tools has sparked an explosion in creativity.

Novel Approaches to Teamwork and Creative Expression:

Additionally, new forms of creative expression and collaboration have been made possible by the digital revolution. Regardless of where they are physically located, creators can now collaborate on remix projects thanks to online platforms and collaborative tools. Global remix communities have emerged as a result, allowing people from various cultures and backgrounds to work together to produce original and inventive works.

Additionally, new kinds of creative expression that were not feasible prior to the digital age have been made possible by digital tools. For instance, remixing components from various media is a common practice in interactive installations, digital art projects, and video games to provide users with immersive and captivating experiences.

Remixing has seen significant change as a result of the digital revolution, which has increased its accessibility, scale, and scope. A new era of creative expression has been ushered in by the tools and technologies of the digital age, which have enabled people to create, share, and collaborate in novel and creative ways. The digital revolution has radically changed remix culture, making it a potent force in modern creativity. This includes everything from digital sampling and manipulation to the internet as a platform for remixes and the democratization of creative tools.

2.1 Digital Technology's Emergence and Effect on Remixing

Remixing has undergone an irreversible transformation since the introduction of digital technologies, which have increased its accessibility, reach, and creative potential. Although the fundamental idea of remixing—combining preexisting elements to create something new—predates the digital era, the tools and platforms developed during the digital revolution have drastically changed the way we produce, distribute, and consume remixed content. The significant influence of digital technologies on remixing will be examined in this essay, along with how these developments have democratized creativity, encouraged new kinds of teamwork and reshaped our conceptions of originality and authorship.

From Analog Restraints to Digital Profusion

Due to the limitations of analog media, remixing was frequently a time-consuming and technically difficult process prior to the digital revolution. For example, sampling in music required physically cutting and splicing magnetic tape, which was a laborious and inaccurate process. Collage and photomontage in the visual arts required painstaking manual labor. Remixing was limited by these analog methods to people with expensive equipment and specialized skills.

These constraints were broken by digital technologies. Creators now have strong and intuitive tools for working with media thanks to the development of digital audio workstations (DAWs), image editing programs like Photoshop, and video editing programs like Final Cut Pro and Adobe Premiere Pro. These tools made it simple to apply effects and transformations, integrate various elements seamlessly, and edit with accuracy. Additionally, the digital environment made non-destructive editing possible, which allowed for experimentation and revisions while preserving the original source material.

The process of democratizing creativity

The democratization of creativity has been one of the biggest effects of digital technologies on remixing. Digital tools' accessibility and affordability have reduced entry barriers, enabling people from all walks of life to engage in remix culture. Remixing was no longer limited to specialized workshops or professional studios; it was now a practice available to anybody with a computer and an internet connection.

A vast amount of creative output has resulted from this democratization, with innumerable people producing and disseminating their remixed content online. Remix culture has flourished thanks to websites like Vimeo, SoundCloud, and YouTube, which give artists access to a worldwide audience and promote a thriving creative community.

The Internet as a Platform for Remixing:

With its extensive computer network and ability to share information quickly, the internet has emerged as a crucial platform for remixing. The internet has become a vast collaborative platform for remix culture due to the ease with which digital content can be copied, shared, and distributed.

New types of remixing that were not feasible in the pre-digital age have been made possible by online platforms. For instance, internet memes, which frequently entail the modification and reworking of preexisting images or phrases, have proliferated as a means of cultural expression and online communication. As they are shared and reinterpreted by various users, these memes change and evolve as they go viral online.

Additionally, the internet has made it possible for artists from all over the world to collaborate on remix projects. File sharing, idea sharing, and co-creation of remixed content have all been made easier by online platforms and collaborative tools.

Novel Remixing Techniques:

In addition to making remixing easier, digital technologies have opened up completely new avenues for artistic expression.

Among the noteworthy instances are:

Mashups: To make a new song, two or more existing songs' elements are combined. This technique, which combines genres and produces surprising juxtapositions, was made popular by digital audio editing software and has since become a mainstay of remix culture.

Video remixes: These techniques entail modifying and rearranging preexisting video content to produce fresh interpretations or stories. These remixes, which can vary from straightforward edits to intricate visual collages, frequently recontextualize the original content through comedy, satire, or commentary.

Fans create new stories or artwork based on pre-existing fictional universes as part of fan fiction and fan art, two types of creative expression made possible by digital tools and online platforms. Alternative plotlines, character interactions, or interpretations of the source material are frequently explored in fan fiction and fan art.

Music production has been transformed by digital samplers and software, which enable musicians to use short clips from pre-existing recordings to create new songs. This method has emerged as a key component of dance music, electronic music, and hip-hop.

Redefining Originality and Authorship:

Important queries concerning authorship and originality have also been brought up by the development of digital technologies. The conventional idea of the lone author as the only creator is called into question in a remix culture where works are frequently produced by combining and reinterpreting preexisting material.

Remixers play an important role because they are not just replicating existing works; they are also reworking and rearranging them while incorporating their own artistic vision. This calls into question ownership, intellectual property, and striking a balance between promoting creativity and defending the rights of creators.

Remixing has seen significant change as a result of the digital revolution, which has increased its accessibility, scale, and scope. A new era of creative expression has been ushered in by the tools and technologies of the digital age, which have enabled people to create, share, and collaborate in novel and creative ways. Digital technologies have radically changed remix culture, making it a potent force in modern creativity. This includes the democratization of creative tools, the internet as a platform for remixes, and the rise of new remixing techniques.

2.2 The Development of Digital Manipulation, Looping, and Sampling in Music

With sampling, looping, and digital manipulation becoming essential components of modern music production, the emergence of digital technologies has completely changed the way that music is created and consumed. Digital tools have democratized these techniques, which were previously restricted by analog equipment's limitations, enabling artists to produce fresh and inventive sounds.

Using the Past to Shape the Future through Sampling

A key component of contemporary music is sampling, which is the act of taking a section of an already-recorded song and using it in a new composition. Artists have blended genres and eras by using samples to create new sonic landscapes in everything from hip-hop to electronic music.

Prior to the digital era, sampling was a time-consuming and costly procedure that frequently required physically cutting and splicing magnetic tape. However, the process became much more accessible with the introduction of computer software and digital samplers. Sounds from any source could now be readily sampled, altered, and incorporated into music by artists.

Both the creation and consumption of music have been altered by sampling. Nowadays, listeners are used to hearing well-known sounds in unfamiliar settings, which blurs the distinctions between genres and fosters intertextuality.

Looping: Producing Repeating Textures and Rhythms

In contemporary music, looping—the act of repeating a segment of audio—has also gained popularity. Artists can produce hypnotic and engrossing soundscapes by producing repetitive rhythms and textures.

Tape loops, which were made by physically joining the ends of a piece of magnetic tape, were the first method of looping. But as digital technology advanced, looping became much more accurate and adaptable. It was now simple for artists to construct loops of any length, adjust their pitch and tempo, and layer them to produce intricate rhythmic patterns.

Hip-hop and electronic music are just two of the genres that have been greatly influenced by looping. It has allowed musicians to push the limits of musical expression by producing complex rhythmic patterns and mesmerizing soundscapes.

Digital Manipulation: Creating Unprecedented Sound Changes

Additionally, artists can now manipulate sound in previously unheard-of ways thanks to digital technology. Artists can now precisely adjust the pitch, tempo, timbre, and spatial properties of sound thanks to the development of digital audio workstations (DAWs) and specialized software.

Through the use of digital manipulation techniques, artists are now able to produce sounds that were previously unattainable. Digital manipulation has evolved into a vital tool for contemporary music production, ranging from minor adjustments to drastic changes.

Music Genres Affected

Numerous musical genres have been significantly impacted by sampling, looping, and digital manipulation. For example, sampling has played a significant role in hip-hop, where musicians use samples from a variety of sources to produce original beats and rhythms. These methods have also changed electronic music, with musicians creating intricate and engrossing soundscapes with loops and digital manipulation.

Artists frequently combine elements from various styles to create new and hybrid forms of music, further blurring the boundaries between genres. A rich and varied musical landscape where creativity and experimentation are highly regarded has resulted from the cross-pollination of genres.

Music Production's Democratization

The introduction of digital technologies has altered not only who can create music but also how it is made. Digital tools' accessibility and affordability have democratized music production, enabling anyone to compose and perform music.

Artists are no longer limited to costly studios; they can now produce music of a high caliber from the comfort of their own homes. More people than ever before are able to express themselves through music as a result of this democratization, which has sparked an explosion in creativity.

The emergence of digital manipulation, looping, and sampling has changed the music industry and given musicians the ability to produce fresh, avant-garde sounds. These methods have altered both the production and consumption of music, obfuscating genre boundaries and

fostering a rich and varied musical environment.

The democratization of music production has also had a significant effect, enabling people to share their works with the world and express themselves through music. It will be fascinating to observe how these methods continue to influence music in the future as technology develops.

2.3 The Development of Digital Image Manipulation and Editing

The development of digital technologies has completely changed how we produce, work with, and use images. From graphic design and photography to social media and advertising, digital image editing and manipulation are now commonplace in many industries. The origins of these technologies, their historical evolution, and their significant influence on visual culture will all be covered in this essay.

From Darkroom to Desktop: How Image Editing Has Changed

Image editing was a tedious and time-consuming process that was done in the darkroom prior to the digital revolution. Photographers altered contrast, brightness, and sharpness in negatives and prints through chemical processes. Retouching was a fine art that involved careful handiwork to eliminate flaws or imperfections from a photograph.

Image editing changed in the late 20th century with the introduction of computers and digital imaging technologies. The creation of programs like Adobe Photoshop, which debuted in 1990, gave users access to a strong and adaptable toolkit for digital image manipulation. These tools made it possible to precisely control a number of image parameters, such as composition, color, and tone.

Additionally, digital image editing opened up new avenues for artistic manipulation. Nowadays, it is simple for designers and artists to produce collages, photomontages, and other types of visual remix, fusing and altering preexisting images to produce fresh, frequently fantastical compositions.

The Effect on Photographic

Both professional and amateur photography have been significantly impacted by digital image editing. These days, photographers use digital tools to improve their photos by modifying sharpness, color balance, and exposure. Since digital tools make it possible to make precise and delicate adjustments to skin tone, blemishes, and other imperfections, retouching has become a standard practice in portrait and fashion photography.

Additionally, the distinctions between photography and other visual arts have become more hazy due to digital image editing. In order to combine several photos into a single, seamless image, photographers now frequently use digital tools to create composite images. Photographers can now produce surreal and fantastical images that were previously unattainable thanks to this technique, which has created new avenues for artistic expression.

The Effect on Graphic Design

Graphic design has also been transformed by digital image editing. Designers now produce logos, illustrations, and other visual components for print and the web using digital tools. Combining text, images, and other graphic elements to create intricate and eye-catching designs has never been simpler thanks to digital image editing.

Graphic design has also been significantly impacted by the introduction of vector graphics software. Vector graphics can be resized to any size without sacrificing quality because they are based on mathematical equations rather than pixels. Because of this, logos and other graphic components can now be made for a variety of applications, ranging from small print to large-scale signage.

The Effect on Media and Advertising

Digital image editing has emerged as a crucial tool for media and advertising. Digital tools are used by advertisers to produce visually appealing ads, frequently enhancing the appearance of people or products through image manipulation. Digital image editing is also used by the media to improve news images and other visual content.

Concerns regarding the possibility of deceit and manipulation have been raised by the extensive use of digital image editing in media and advertising. Critics contend that manipulating images with digital tools can lead to harmful stereotypes and inflated expectations.

The Effect on Social Media

Social media has also been significantly impacted by digital image editing. Nowadays, people edit and improve their photos using digital tools before posting them online. The "selfie" culture, in which users frequently post romanticized images of themselves on social media, has grown as a result of this.

Concerns regarding the possibility of body image problems and social comparison have also been raised by the use of digital image editing on social media. Critics contend that low self-esteem and feelings of inadequacy can result from constant exposure to idealized images on social media.

Visual culture has undergone a significant transformation since the advent of digital image editing and manipulation. People can now create and manipulate images more easily than ever before thanks to these technologies, which have democratized creativity. They have nevertheless also sparked worries about the possibility of deceit and manipulation. As digital imaging technologies develop further, it's critical to use them sensibly and to consider how they might affect society.

2.4 The Internet as a Channel for Remixed Content Distribution and Sharing

The way we produce, distribute, and use information has been completely transformed by the internet. Because it offers a large and easily accessible platform for sharing and disseminating remixed content, it has also had a significant influence on remix culture. This paper will investigate the ways in which remix culture has expanded thanks to the internet, looking at how it affects creativity, teamwork, and copyright.

From Platforms for Streaming to File Sharing:

Remixed content distribution and sharing was a challenging and frequently constrained process prior to the internet. It was necessary to make physical copies of music, movies, and other media and distribute them via conventional means like mail order, record stores, and video rental shops. This made it challenging for consumers to access remixed content and for creators to reach a large audience.

All of that has changed because of the internet. In the late 1990s and early 2000s, file-sharing websites like Limewire and Napster appeared, making it simple for users to exchange digital files. As a result, users started making and sharing their own edits, mashups, and remixes, which caused the sharing of remixed music to soar.

Remixed content became even easier to share and consume as new platforms arose as streaming technologies advanced and internet speeds rose. By giving producers a worldwide audience and giving users access to a sizable collection of remixed content, YouTube, SoundCloud, and Vimeo developed into centers of remix culture.

The Development of Virtual Communities:

Online communities devoted to remix culture have also been made possible by the internet. These communities give artists a place to collaborate, share their work, and have conversations about remixing.

Important centers for remix culture now include social media groups, online forums, and websites devoted to remixing. Through these platforms, artists can interact with one another, share their creations, and get input from other remixers. They also give fans a place to interact with the remix community and find new remixed content.

Novel Remixing Techniques:

In addition to making it simpler to share and disseminate remixed content, the internet has made it possible for new kinds of remixing that were not feasible prior to the digital era.

Among the noteworthy instances are:

Internet memes: Memes are a common way for people to communicate and express their culture online. They frequently involve the modification and reworking of preexisting images or phrases. As they are shared and reinterpreted by various users, these memes change and evolve as they go viral online.

Fans create new stories or artwork based on pre-existing fictional universes as part of fan fiction and fan art, two types of creative expression made possible by digital tools and online platforms. Alternative plotlines, character interactions, or interpretations of the source material is frequently explored in fan fiction and fan art.

Video remixes: These techniques entail modifying and rearranging preexisting video content to produce fresh interpretations or stories. These remixes, which can vary from straightforward edits to intricate visual collages, frequently recontextualize the original content through comedy, satire, or commentary.

The Effect on Copyright:

Important concerns regarding copyright and intellectual property have been brought up by the ease with which digital content can be copied and shared online. Remixing and copyright law, which is intended to safeguard creators' rights, can occasionally clash, especially when using copyrighted content without authorization.

When discussing remix culture, the idea of ***"fair use,"*** which permits specific uses of copyrighted content without consent, is frequently brought up. However, there is frequently debate regarding whether a specific remix qualifies as fair use or copyright infringement, and the limits of fair use can be ambiguous.

Remix culture has been significantly changed by the internet, which offers a huge and easily accessible platform for sharing and disseminating remixed content. It has made creativity more accessible, encouraged new kinds of teamwork, and made remixing possible. But it has also brought up significant issues with intellectual property and copyright. Striking a balance between defending the rights of creators and encouraging creativity will be crucial as the internet develops.

2.5 Hardware and Software's Impact on Creative Potential

Software and hardware are the basic tools that allow for creative expression in many different fields. The advancement of these technologies has greatly influenced creative possibilities, pushing the boundaries of what is feasible and creating new channels for expression in fields ranging from writing and filmmaking to the visual arts and music production. This essay will address the effects of hardware and software on creativity as well as how these tools have democratized access, spurred innovation, and changed the creative process.

The democratization of instruments of art

One of the most significant outcomes of hardware and software has been the democratization of creative tools. Before the digital revolution, professional-grade hardware and software were often only available to those with significant financial means or specialized training. However, people from all walks of life can now pursue creative endeavors thanks to the development of affordable computers, user-friendly software, and accessible hardware.

Previously exclusive to professional designers, software such as Adobe Photoshop is now accessible to anyone with a computer. Similarly, programs like GarageBand and Ableton Live have made it possible for aspiring musicians to record professionally from the comfort of their own homes. The democratization of creative tools has made it possible for more people than ever before to express themselves through a range of artistic mediums.

Enhanced Precision and Ingenuity:

Furthermore, artists now have unprecedented levels of control and accuracy over their work thanks to hardware and software. Artists were often limited by the physical constraints of their tools. For instance, painters needed to use their hand-eye coordination and mix their own colors in order to apply paint to a canvas.

Digital tools have removed many of these limitations. Using graphic design software, artists can create precise shapes, lines, and colors with a few mouse clicks. Music production software makes it simple for musicians to adjust pitch, tempo, and timbre, allowing them to work with sound with remarkable accuracy. The greater control and precision that have opened up new channels for artistic expression have allowed artists to realize their ideas with greater accuracy and detail.

Novel Techniques for Creative Expression:

Additionally, the development of hardware and software has enabled entirely new forms of creative expression that were not possible before the digital age.

Among the notable examples are:

Digital art: Tools such as Photoshop and Illustrator have enabled the creation of digital paintings, illustrations, and other forms of visual art. Artists can create intricate and stunning artwork with the range of brushes, colors, and effects these tools offer.

Computer-generated imagery (CGI), enabled by specialized software and powerful hardware, has revolutionized video games, animation, and filmmaking. Artists can create realistic or fantastical images and animations using computer-generated imagery (CGI), creating visually stunning and engrossing experiences.

Virtual reality (VR) and augmented reality (AR) technologies have opened up new possibilities for immersive and interactive storytelling with the aid of state-of-the-art hardware and software. These technologies allow artists to create virtual worlds and experiences that blur the lines between reality and fiction.

Collaboration and Communication:

Additionally, hardware and software have enabled new forms of creator sharing and collaboration. Thanks to online platforms and collaborative tools, artists, musicians, writers, and filmmakers can now work together on projects regardless of where they are physically located.

Cloud storage services and file-sharing platforms have made it easy to share files and collaborate on projects in real time. Artists can now interact with their audience, share their work, and receive feedback thanks to social media platforms.

The Impact on Specific Creative Domains:

Numerous fields illustrate how software and hardware impact creative potential:

Music: Software such as Logic Pro X and Ableton Live has transformed music production by allowing musicians to create complex, multi-layered compositions from the convenience of their own homes. Thanks to devices like MIDI controllers and synthesizers, musicians can now access a greater variety of sounds.

Visual arts: Photoshop and Illustrator are now essential tools for graphic designers, photographers, and illustrators. Hardware that has enhanced the creative process includes drawing tablets and high-resolution monitors.

Writing: Word processing software and online writing platforms have made it easier for writers to produce, edit, and distribute their work. Thanks to gadgets like laptops and tablets, writers are now more mobile and flexible.

Filmmaking: It is now possible to create high-quality films with smaller crews and budgets because of developments in digital cameras, editing software, and special effects software.

Both hardware and software have significantly changed the creative possibilities. They have democratized access to creative tools, enhanced creative control and accuracy, created new channels for creative expression, and facilitated collaboration and idea sharing. As technology advances, it will be interesting to see how these tools continue to inspire creativity.

Chapter 3:

Copyright and Creativity: The Remix Dilemma

The relationship between copyright and creativity has grown more complicated in the digital age, as media and information can be readily shared, altered, and copied. Remixing, which is the process of using preexisting works to create something new, can occasionally clash with copyright laws, which are intended to safeguard creators' rights. The remix dilemma will be examined in this essay, along with the conflict between creativity and copyright and the different viewpoints on this intricate matter.

Why Copyright Is Important

Authors, artists, musicians, and dramatists are all granted exclusive rights to their original works by copyright law. These rights cover the reproduction, distribution, performance, and exhibition of the work. By guaranteeing that creators receive compensation for their work; copyright protection aims to encourage creativity.

Additionally, copyright law contains restrictions and exceptions, such as fair use, which permits specific unapproved uses of copyrighted content. The goal of fair use is to strike a balance between the public interest in encouraging creativity and innovation and the rights of creators.

Remix Culture's Ascent

Remix culture has emerged as a result of the development of digital technologies, in which people utilize preexisting works to produce original, transformative works. Fan fiction, video editing, and music sampling are just a few of the various ways that remixing can be done.

The ease of copying, sharing, and altering digital content has been a driving force behind remix culture. Another important factor has been the internet, which gives artists a place to share their creations and work together.

The Conflict Between Creativity and Copyright

The practice of remixing and copyright law are at odds as a result of the growth of remix culture. By limiting the use of previously created works, copyright laws, which are intended to safeguard creators' rights, can occasionally be perceived as impeding creativity.

Remixers frequently contend that their work is transformative and does not violate copyright holders' rights. They contend that because their use of preexisting works is transformative and does not negatively impact the original work's market, it qualifies as fair use.

Nonetheless, copyright owners frequently contend that remixing does violate their rights. They contend that remixers are undermining their ability to make money off of their creations by using their work without their consent.

Striking a Balance

It can be difficult to strike a balance between copyright protection and encouraging creativity. Some contend that in order to safeguard the rights of creators, copyright should be applied more strictly. Others contend that a more adaptable strategy is required to foster innovation and creativity.

Extending the definition of fair use is one way to strike a balance. As long as the use is transformative and does not negatively impact the original work's market, this would permit more unapproved uses of copyrighted content.

Creating alternative licensing models, like Creative Commons licenses, is an additional strategy. With these licenses, authors can give others specific permissions while keeping some of their own rights.

The conflict between copyright and creativity in the digital age is exemplified by the remix dilemma. Finding a balance between protecting the rights of creators and promoting creativity is a complex issue with no easy answers. However, by engaging in thoughtful and nuanced discussion, we can find solutions that promote both copyright protection and creativity.

I would like to add the following to the previously mentioned:

The remix conundrum is a cultural problem in addition to a legal one. It's critical to take into account how copyright laws may affect culture and make sure they don't inhibit innovation.
As technology advances, the remix dilemma will continue to be a problem. To make sure that copyright law is still applicable and useful, it is critical that discussions about this topic continue.
I hope this essay has clarified the remix conundrum and the conflict between creativity and copyright.

3.1 Examining the legal framework of copyright and its implications for remix culture.

Remix culture and copyright law, a legal framework intended to safeguard creators' rights, have a complicated and frequently tense relationship. By definition, remixing is the process of creating new, transformative works by utilizing previously published copyrighted works. In-depth discussion of the fundamental ideas of copyright law and its consequences for the remixing industry will be provided in this essay.

Important Copyright Law Principles:

Authors, artists, musicians, and dramatists are all granted exclusive rights to their original works by copyright law. These rights include the ability to make derivative works based on the copyrighted work and to reproduce, distribute, perform, and display it.

Copyright law is based on several fundamental ideas:

Originality: Only original works of authorship are protected by copyright. This implies that the author must have produced the work on their own and with only a small amount of originality.

Expression: An idea's expression, not the idea itself, is protected by copyright. This implies that as long as they express the same ideas in a different way, others are free to use them.

Restricted time: The protection of copyright is not indefinite. It lasts for a certain amount of time, after which the work becomes public domain and is available for use by anybody.

A legal principle known as *"fair use"* permits some uses of content protected by copyright without the owner's consent. This theory aims to strike a balance between the public interest in encouraging creativity and innovation and the rights of creators.

Consequences for Remix Culture:

Remix culture is significantly impacted by the copyright legal framework. Remixing may violate copyright holders' rights since it frequently entails using protected content without their consent.

Nonetheless, remixers are given some wiggle room under the fair use doctrine. Fair use permits the use of copyrighted content for educational, parodic, critical, and commentary purposes.

Courts take into account four factors when deciding whether a given use qualifies as fair use:

The use's intent and nature: This element takes into account whether the use is transformative—that is, whether it gives the original work a new meaning or expression—as well as whether it is commercial or noncommercial.

The type of work being used, whether it is factual or creative, and whether it has been published before are all taken into account by the copyrighted work's nature.

The quantity and significance of the portion used: This factor takes into account the amount of the copyrighted work that was used as well as whether the portion was central to the work.

The impact of the use on the copyrighted work's potential market or value: This factor takes into account whether the use hurts the market for the original work or its derivatives.

Difficulties and Debates:

There has been much discussion and disagreement regarding the application of copyright law to remix culture. Some contend that because copyright laws restrict remixers' use of previously created works, they are overly restrictive and stifle creativity. Others contend that in order to safeguard creators' rights and guarantee that they receive payment for their labor, copyright legislation is necessary.

Determining whether a specific remix is transformative enough to be considered fair use is one of the major challenges. Courts must conduct this intricate and fact-specific investigation on an individual basis.

The ambiguity surrounding the parameters of fair use in the digital sphere presents another difficulty. The ease with which copyrighted content can now be copied and shared online has raised worries about copyright infringement.

Remix culture is significantly impacted by copyright laws. Although the purpose of copyright law is to safeguard the rights of creators, remixers who utilize preexisting works to produce original, transformative works may encounter difficulties as a result. Although the fair use doctrine offers some leeway, it is frequently difficult and controversial to apply to remix culture.

It's never easy to strike a balance between fostering creativity and defending creators' rights. It necessitates a sophisticated comprehension of copyright legislation and how it affects remix culture. It will be crucial to review and reevaluate the copyright legal framework as technology develops further to make sure it is still applicable and useful in the digital era.

3.2 The Argument Between Transformative and Fair Use

The ongoing discussion about copyright law and its application in the digital age, especially with regard to remix culture and other creative re-use practices, revolves around the concepts of fair use and transformative use. These legal theories make an effort to strike a balance between the public interest in encouraging creativity, innovation, free speech, and the rights of copyright holders. Nonetheless, these doctrines' interpretation and application are frequently difficult and divisive, sparking continuous discussion and legal issues.

Fair Use: An Act of Balance

A legal principle known as *"fair use"* permits the restricted use of copyrighted content for specific purposes—such as research, teaching, scholarship, news reporting, criticism, and commentary—without the owner's consent. In the US, it is enshrined in Section 107 of the Copyright Act of 1976.

A four-factor test is used to determine whether a given use is considered fair use:

The use's character and purpose: This element takes into account whether the use is transformative and whether it is commercial or noncommercial. One important component of this factor is transformative use, which is covered below.

The type of work being used, whether it is factual or creative, and whether it has been published before are all taken into account by the copyrighted work's nature.

How much of the copyrighted work was used and whether the portion was the *"heart"* of the work are two factors that are taken into account by the amount and substantiality of the portion used.

The impact of the use on the copyrighted work's potential market or value: This factor takes into account whether the use hurts the market for the original work or its derivatives.

No one of these four factors is decisive; instead, they are all considered in a balancing test. Given the particular facts of each case, courts must take all the factors into account.

Adding a new meaning or purpose is known as transformative use.

One of the main ideas of the fair use doctrine is transformative use. A transformative use is one that gives the original work a new meaning, expression, or objective. It's not just a copy or a derivative that adheres closely to the original.

The significance of transformative use in fair use analysis was established by the Supreme Court's ruling in Campbell v. Acuff-Rose Music, Inc. (1994). The rap group 2 Live Crew parodied the Roy Orbison song *"Oh, Pretty Woman"* in the case. Because the parody gave the original song new insight and commentary, the Court determined that it was a transformative use.

In the context of remix culture, the idea of transformative use has gained significant attention. Remixes frequently entail taking preexisting works and turning them into brand-new, unique works. One of the most important questions in copyright disputes is whether a specific remix counts as transformative use.

The Argument and Difficulties:

There has been much discussion and disagreement regarding how fair use and transformative use should be interpreted and applied. It can be challenging for creators to determine whether their use of copyrighted content will be deemed fair use due to the fair use doctrine's ambiguity and unpredictability, according to some. Others contend that an unduly expansive interpretation of fair use has resulted from the emphasis on transformative use, permitting uses that are detrimental to the market for original works.

Determining what a transformative use is is one of the major challenges. There isn't a precise definition, and courts have approached this problem in various ways. Different courts have focused on whether the use is for a different purpose than the original work, while others have focused on whether the use adds a new meaning or message.

Applying the four-factor fair use test in a digital setting presents another difficulty. New concerns regarding the quantity and quality of the portion used, as well as the impact on the original work's market, have been brought up by the ease with which digital content can be copied and shared.

Case Studies and Examples:

The argument between fair use and transformative use has been brought to light by a number of well-known cases:

Google's scanning of millions of books to build a digital library was at issue in the Authors Guild v. Google case. Because it was transformative, opening up new information sources and research opportunities, the courts ruled that this use qualified as fair use.
The case Perfect 10, Inc. v. Amazon.com, Inc. concerned Google's use of copyrighted photo

thumbnails in its search results. Because this use was transformative and served a different purpose than the original photographs, the courts ruled that it was fair use.

These instances highlight the difficulties in implementing transformative use and fair use in the digital sphere.

The balance between copyright protection and the encouragement of creativity is a topic of continuous and significant discussion in the context of fair use and transformative use. By permitting specific uses of copyrighted content that serve the public interest, these doctrines seek to give copyright law some leeway. Nonetheless, these doctrines' interpretation and application are frequently difficult and divisive, sparking continuous discussion and legal issues. The discussion of fair use and transformative use will remain a crucial aspect of the copyright environment as long as technology advances and new creative expression mediums appear.

3.3 Examples of Copyright Conflicts Concerning Remixed Works

In the digital age, disputes over remixed works have become more common in the field of copyright law. The conflict between defending the rights of original creators and encouraging creativity through transformative use is frequently at the center of these cases. Let's examine a few noteworthy case studies that illustrate the subtleties and complexity of this legal environment.

Acuff-Rose Music, Inc. v. Campbell (1994)

In this court case, 2 Live Crew parodied Roy Orbison's song *"Oh, Pretty Woman."* Because it gave the original work new meaning and commentary, the Supreme Court decided that 2 Live Crew's rendition was a transformative use. The significance of transformative use in fair use analysis was established by this ruling.

Dimension Films v. Bridgeport Music, Inc. (2005)

In this instance, the N.W.A. song *"100 Miles and Runnin'"* featured a two-second guitar riff from Funkadelic's *"Get Off Your Ass and Jam."* The court established a stringent standard for sampling in music, ruling that even a brief sample could amount to copyright infringement.

Prince v. Cariou (2013)

In this instance, Patrick Cariou's photographs were used by artist Richard Prince for his *"Canal Zone"* series. Because Prince had not significantly altered the original works' expression or meaning, the court determined that his use of the photographs was not transformative. The significance of proving transformative use in fair use claims was emphasized by this ruling.

Google v. Authors Guild (2013)

In this instance, Google created a digital library by scanning millions of books. Because Google's use of the books was revolutionary and opened up new information sources, the court decided that it was fair use. The significance of fair use in fostering access to information and research was upheld by this ruling.

Amazon.com, Inc. v. Perfect 10, Inc. (2007)

In this case, Google's search results included thumbnails of photos that were protected by copyright. Because Google's use of the photos was transformative and had a different purpose than the original photos, the court decided that it was fair use. This ruling brought the significance of fair use in facilitating new technologies and online services to light.

Important Takeaways

The intricacies of copyright disputes involving remixed works are demonstrated by these case studies. Different methods have been used by the courts to decide whether a given use qualifies as fair use, and the results of each case vary depending on the particular facts. Nonetheless, these cases highlight some important lessons:

A crucial component of fair use analysis is transformative use.
Copyright violations can occur from even brief samples.
Fair use can apply to new technologies and online services.
Applying fair use is a fact-specific investigation.
The Ongoing Discussion

Fair use and transformative use are still up for debate. There is no clear consensus on how these doctrines should be applied in all cases.

Uncertainty and legal action have resulted from this, especially in relation to remix culture.

Some argue that the current legal framework is too restrictive and stifles creativity. They support a more accommodating strategy that would permit more unapproved use of copyrighted content. Others contend that in order to safeguard creators' rights and guarantee their payment for their labor, the current framework is required.

It can be difficult to strike a balance between fostering creativity and defending the rights of creators. It necessitates a sophisticated comprehension of copyright legislation and how it affects remix culture. It will be crucial to review and reevaluate the copyright legal framework as technology develops further to make sure it is still applicable and useful in the digital era.

This essay's case studies demonstrate the subtleties and complexity of copyright disputes involving remixed works. Different methods have been used by the courts to decide whether a given use qualifies as fair use, and the results of each case vary depending on the particular facts. In order to guarantee that copyright law is still applicable and useful in the digital age, it is critical to keep up the ongoing discussion about fair use and transformative use.

3.4 The Function of Alternative Licensing Models, Including Creative Commons

Traditional copyright law has struggled to strike a balance between creators' rights and the public interest in encouraging creativity and innovation in the digital age, where creative works can be readily copied, shared, and altered. In response to these difficulties, alternative licensing models such as Creative Commons have surfaced, providing authors with an easy-to-use and adaptable method of controlling the copyright of their creations while promoting sharing and cooperation.

Creative Commons: A Range of Authorizations

A non-profit organization called Creative Commons (CC) offers free legal tools that let creators give the public specific permissions while keeping some rights. A range of permissions are provided by CC licenses, from permitting all uses with attribution to permitting only noncommercial uses devoid of derivatives.

CC licenses have four primary requirements, which are:

Attribution (BY): This requirement mandates that users acknowledge the original author.
Users must license their derivative works under the same terms as the original work in order to comply with the ShareAlike (SA) condition.

NonCommercial (NC): Users are prohibited from using the work for profit under this condition.

NoDerivatives (ND): Users are not allowed to create derivative works under this condition.

Six primary CC licenses can be created by combining these requirements:

As long as the original creator is credited, users are free to use the work for any purpose, including commercial ones, under the CC BY license.

As long as users give due credit to the original creator and license their derivative works under the same terms, they are permitted to use the work for any purpose, including commercial ones, under the CC BY-SA license.

Under the CC BY-NC license, users are only permitted to use the work for noncommercial purposes as long as they acknowledge the original author.

Users may only use the work for noncommercial purposes under the terms of the CC BY-NC-SA license, provided that they give due credit to the original author and grant the same license to their derivative works.

As long as users give credit to the original creator and refrain from creating derivative works, they are permitted to use the work for any purpose, including commercial ones, under the CC BY-ND license.

Under the terms of the CC BY-NC-ND license, users may only use the work for noncommercial purposes as long as they acknowledge the original author and refrain from producing derivative works.

Other Models of Alternative Licensing:

Other alternative licensing models have surfaced in addition to Creative Commons, providing distinct methods for copyright management:

Software is frequently licensed under the GNU General Public License (GPL), which mandates that derivative works be open source and subject to the same conditions.

Copyleft is a broad term that refers to the use of copyright legislation to guarantee that artistic creations are always accessible and that others are free to alter and distribute them.

The Open Source Initiative (OSI) encourages the free distribution, access, and modification of software by certifying licenses that adhere to the Open Source Definition.

Advantages of Different License Models:

For both the public and creators, alternative licensing models provide a number of advantages:

Flexibility: They give authors a variety of choices for controlling the copyright of their creations, enabling them to decide how much public access they wish to grant.

Accessibility: They encourage creativity and innovation by making it simpler for the general public to use and share creative works.

Cooperation: They promote cooperation and the production of derivative works, which results in fresh and creative works.

Noncommercial use: They give authors the ability to permit noncommercial uses of their creations while maintaining authority over commercial ones.

Obstacles and Restrictions:

There are certain restrictions and difficulties with alternative licensing models as well.

Enforcement: These licenses can be challenging to enforce, especially when it comes to online infringement.
Understanding: The public may not fully understand the terms of these licenses, leading to confusion and misuse.
Commercial use: Some creators may be hesitant to use licenses that allow commercial use, as they may want to retain exclusive control over the commercial exploitation of their works.

Creative Commons and other alternative licensing models have played a significant role in promoting remix culture and fostering creativity in the digital age. They offer a flexible and accessible way for creators to manage the copyright of their works while encouraging sharing and collaboration. While these models face some challenges and limitations, they represent an important step towards balancing the rights of creators with the public interest in promoting creativity and innovation. Alternative licensing models will probably continue to be crucial in determining how copyright and artistic expression are shaped in the future as technology advances.

3.5 The Conflict Between Encouraging Creativity and Preserving the Rights of Creators

In addition to offering previously unheard-of chances for creativity and innovation, the digital age has also presented new difficulties for defending creators' rights. Remix culture, which thrives on the use of preexisting works, and copyright law, which is intended to protect creators, are at odds because of how easily digital content can be copied, shared, and altered.

Copyright Law: Juggling Incentives and Rights

Authors, artists, musicians, and dramatists are all granted exclusive rights to their original works by copyright law. These rights cover the reproduction, distribution, performance, and exhibition of the work. By guaranteeing that creators receive compensation for their work, copyright protection aims to encourage creativity.

Additionally, copyright law contains restrictions and exceptions, such as fair use, which permits specific unapproved uses of copyrighted content. The goal of fair use is to strike a balance between the public interest in encouraging creativity and innovation and the rights of creators.

Remix Culture: Innovation via Metamorphosis

A creative movement known as remix culture uses preexisting works to produce fresh, revolutionary works. Fan fiction, video editing, and music sampling are just a few of the various ways that remixing can be done.

The ease of copying, sharing, and altering digital content has been a driving force behind remix culture. Another important factor has been the internet, which gives artists a place to share their creations and work together.

The Tension: Differing Objectives

The practice of remixing and copyright law are at odds as a result of the growth of remix culture. By limiting the use of previously created works, copyright laws, which are intended to safeguard creators' rights, can occasionally be perceived as impeding creativity.

Remixers frequently contend that their work is transformative and does not violate copyright holders' rights. They contend that because their use of preexisting works is transformative and does not negatively impact the original work's market, it qualifies as fair use.

Nonetheless, copyright owners frequently contend that remixing does violate their rights. They contend that remixers are undermining their ability to make money off of their creations by using their work without their consent.

Striking a Balance: A Difficult Task

It can be difficult to strike a balance between copyright protection and encouraging creativity. Some contend that in order to safeguard the rights of creators, copyright should be applied more strictly. Others contend that a more adaptable strategy is required to foster innovation and creativity.

Extending the definition of fair use is one way to strike a balance. As long as the use is transformative and does not negatively impact the original work's market, this would permit more unapproved uses of copyrighted content.

Creating alternative licensing models, like Creative Commons licenses, is an additional strategy. With these licenses, authors can give others specific permissions while keeping some of their own rights.

A Continuous Discussion

There are no simple solutions to the complex problem of balancing the rights of creators with encouraging creativity. To guarantee that the public and creators can both profit from the digital era, it is critical to have a careful and nuanced conversation about this matter.

I would like to add the following to the previously mentioned:

In addition to being a legal concern, the conflict between upholding the rights of creators and encouraging creativity is also a cultural one. It's critical to take into account how copyright laws may affect culture and make sure they don't inhibit innovation.

As technology advances, the conflict between upholding the rights of creators and encouraging creativity will only intensify. To make sure that copyright law is still applicable and useful, it is critical that discussions about this topic continue.

I hope this essay has clarified the conflict between promoting creativity and defending the rights of creators.

Chapter 4:

Music Remixed: From Sampling to Mashups

Remixing has changed how we make, listen to, and enjoy music. It started with simple sampling and has since progressed to intricate mashups. The development of music remixing will be examined in this essay, from the earliest sampling methods to the emergence of remixups and other modern remix formats.

The Basis of Remix Culture: Sampling

A key component of contemporary music is sampling, which is the act of taking a section of an already-recorded song and using it in a new composition. Artists have blended genres and eras by using samples to create new sonic landscapes in everything from hip-hop to electronic music.

Prior to the digital era, sampling was a time-consuming and costly procedure that frequently required physically cutting and splicing magnetic tape. However, the process became much more accessible with the introduction of computer software and digital samplers. Sounds from any source could now be readily sampled, altered, and incorporated into music by artists.

Both the creation and consumption of music have been altered by sampling. Nowadays, listeners are used to hearing well-known sounds in unfamiliar settings, which blurs the distinctions between genres and fosters intertextuality.

Looping: Producing Repeating Textures and Rhythms

In contemporary music, looping—the act of repeating a segment of audio—has also gained popularity. Artists can produce hypnotic and engrossing soundscapes by producing repetitive rhythms and textures.

Tape loops, which were made by physically joining the ends of a piece of magnetic tape, were the first method of looping. But as digital technology advanced, looping became much more accurate and adaptable. It was now simple for artists to construct loops of any length, adjust their pitch and tempo, and layer them to produce intricate rhythmic patterns.

Hip-hop and electronic music are just two of the genres that have been greatly influenced by looping. It has allowed musicians to push the limits of musical expression by producing complex rhythmic patterns and mesmerizing soundscapes.

Digital Manipulation: Creating Unprecedented Sound Changes

Additionally, artists can now manipulate sound in previously unheard-of ways thanks to digital technology. Artists can now precisely adjust the pitch, tempo, timbre, and spatial properties of sound thanks to the development of digital audio workstations (DAWs) and specialized software.

Through the use of digital manipulation techniques, artists are now able to produce sounds that were previously unattainable. Digital manipulation has evolved into a vital tool for contemporary music production, ranging from minor adjustments to drastic changes.

Mashups' Ascent: Merging Genres and Time Periods

Mashups are a more recent type of remixing in which two or more songs' elements are combined to create a new song. This technique, which combines genres and produces surprising juxtapositions, was made popular by digital audio editing software and has since become a mainstay of remix culture.

In a mashup, the vocals of one song are frequently combined with the instrumental track of another to create a novel and frequently unexpected combination. Artists have been able to produce original and inventive songs that combine various genres and historical periods thanks to this technique.

Music Genres Affected

Digital manipulation, mashups, looping, and sampling have all had a significant influence on different musical genres. For example, sampling has played a significant role in hip-hop, where musicians use samples from a variety of sources to produce original beats and rhythms. These methods have also changed electronic music, with musicians creating intricate and engrossing soundscapes with loops and digital manipulation.

Artists frequently combine elements from various styles to create new and hybrid forms of music, further blurring the boundaries between genres. A rich and varied musical landscape where creativity and experimentation are highly regarded has resulted from the cross-pollination of genres.

Music Production's Democratization

The introduction of digital technologies has altered not only who can create music but also how it is made. Digital tools' accessibility and affordability have democratized music production, enabling anyone to compose and perform music.

Artists are no longer limited to costly studios; they can now produce music of a high caliber from the comfort of their own homes. More people than ever before are able to express themselves through music as a result of this democratization, which has sparked an explosion in creativity.

From sampling to mashups, the development of music remixing has changed the musical landscape and enabled musicians to produce fresh, avant-garde sounds. These methods have altered both the production and consumption of music, obfuscating genre boundaries and fostering a rich and varied musical environment.

The democratization of music production has also had a significant effect, enabling people to share their works with the world and express themselves through music. It will be fascinating to observe how these methods continue to influence music in the future as technology develops.

4.1 Examining the Development and History of Music Remixing

From straightforward sampling to intricate mashups, the craft of remixing music has transformed how we produce, listen to, and enjoy music. The development of music remixing will be examined in this essay, from the earremixupsampling methods to the emergence of mashups and other modern remix formats.

The Basis of Remix Culture: Sampling

A key component of contemporary music is sampling, which is the act of taking a section of an already-recorded song and using it in a new composition. Artists have blended genres and eras by using samples to create new sonic landscapes in everything from hip-hop to electronic music.

Prior to the digital era, sampling was a time-consuming and costly procedure that frequently required physically cutting and splicing magnetic tape. However, the process became much more accessible with the introduction of computer software and digital samplers. Sounds from any source could now be readily sampled, altered, and incorporated into music by artists.

Both the creation and consumption of music have been altered by sampling. Nowadays, listeners are used to hearing well-known sounds in unfamiliar settings, which blurs the distinctions between genres and fosters intertextuality.

Looping: Producing Repeating Textures and Rhythms

In contemporary music, looping—the act of repeating a segment of audio—has also gained popularity. Artists can produce hypnotic and engrossing soundscapes by producing repetitive rhythms and textures.

Tape loops, which were made by physically joining the ends of a piece of magnetic tape, were the first method of looping. But as digital technology advanced, looping became much more accurate and adaptable. It was now simple for artists to construct loops of any length, adjust their pitch and tempo, and layer them to produce intricate rhythmic patterns.

Hip-hop and electronic music are just two of the genres that have been greatly influenced by looping. It has allowed musicians to push the limits of musical expression by producing complex rhythmic patterns and mesmerizing soundscapes.

Digital Manipulation: Creating Unprecedented Sound Changes

Additionally, artists can now manipulate sound in previously unheard-of ways thanks to digital technology. Artists can now precisely adjust the pitch, tempo, timbre, and spatial properties of sound thanks to the development of digital audio workstations (DAWs) and specialized software.

Through the use of digital manipulation techniques, artists are now able to produce sounds that were previously unattainable. Digital manipulation has evolved into a vital tool for contemporary music production, ranging from minor adjustments to drastic changes.

Mashups' Ascent: Merging Genres and Time Periods

Mashups are a more recent type of remixing in which two or more songs' elements are combined to create a new song. This technique, which combines genres and produces surprising juxtapositions, was made popular by digital audio editing software and has since become a mainstay of remix culture.

In a mashup, the vocals of one song are frequently combined with the instrumental track of another to create a novel and frequently unexpected combination. Artists have been able to produce original and inventive songs that combine various genres and historical periods thanks to this technique.

Music Genres Affected

Digital manipulation, mashups, looping, and sampling have all had a significant influence on different musical genres. For example, sampling has played a significant role in hip-hop, where musicians use samples from a variety of sources to produce original beats and rhythms. These methods have also changed electronic music, with musicians creating intricate and engrossing soundscapes with loops and digital manipulation.

Artists frequently combine elements from various styles to create new and hybrid forms of music, further blurring the boundaries between genres. A rich and varied musical landscape where creativity and experimentation are highly regarded has resulted from the cross-pollination of genres.

Music Production's Democratization

The introduction of digital technologies has altered not only who can create music but also how it is made. Digital tools' accessibility and affordability have democratized music production, enabling anyone to compose and perform music.

Artists are no longer limited to costly studios; they can now produce music of a high caliber from the comfort of their own homes. More people than ever before are able to express themselves through music as a result of this democratization, which has sparked an explosion in creativity.

From sampling to mashups, the development of music remixing has changed the musical landscape and enabled musicians to produce fresh, avant-garde sounds. These methods have altered both the production and consumption of music, obfuscating genre boundaries and

fostering a rich and varied musical environment.

The democratization of music production has also had a significant effect, enabling people to share their works with the world and express themselves through music. It will be fascinating to observe how these methods continue to influence music in the future as technology develops.

4.2 Hip-hop and Electronic Music's Effect on Remix Culture

Remix culture has been greatly influenced by hip-hop and electronic music, which has expanded the possibilities for musical expression and changed how we make, listen to, and enjoy music. The significant influence that these two genres have had an impact on remix culture and will be discussed in this essay, along with how they have developed novel methods, questioned conventional ideas of authorship, and promoted an innovative reuse culture.

Hip-Hop: The Skill of Recontextualization and Sampling

The practice of sampling is fundamental to hip hop, which first appeared in the Bronx of New York City in the 1970s. In order to create rhythmic bases for MCs to rap over, DJs started separating and looping drum breaks from already-released records. This method, referred to as **"breakbeat DJing,"** established the foundation for contemporary sampling.

Samplers became increasingly complex as technology advanced, enabling musicians to capture not only drum breaks but also vocals, melodies, and other acoustic components. As a result, intricate and multi-layered compositions incorporating elements from different genres and eras were produced.

In hip-hop, sampling is about recontextualizing sounds rather than merely stealing them. In order to add their own unique creative spin to preexisting material, artists frequently utilize samples to generate new meanings and juxtapositions. Numerous classic hip-hop songs that are based on samples from jazz, funk, soul, and other genres have been produced as a result of this practice.

Conventional ideas of authorship have also been questioned by hip-hop. In a genre where sampling is common, it can be difficult to distinguish between original work and reuse. This has sparked discussions regarding intellectual property and copyright, but it has also promoted a creative reuse culture in which artists are urged to expand on the work of others.

The Influence of Looping and Digital Manipulation in Electronic Music

Remix culture has also been greatly influenced by electronic music, which includes a broad variety of genres like house, techno, and trance. In order to produce recurring rhythms and textures, early electronic musicians experimented with tape loops and other analog techniques.

Looping became considerably more accurate and adaptable with the introduction of digital technology. It was now simple for artists to construct loops of any length, adjust their pitch and tempo, and layer them to produce intricate rhythmic patterns.

Digital technology also made it possible to manipulate sound in new ways. In order to produce fresh and inventive sounds, artists started utilizing synthesizers, effects processors, and other digital instruments. As a result, new electronic music genres and subgenres emerged, each with distinctive acoustic traits.

Remixing has also become popular in electronic music, with musicians reworking popular songs to create something completely different from the original. These remixes demonstrate the versatility of electronic music production techniques, ranging from subtle edits to radical reinterpretations.

Hip-hop and Electronic Music's Convergence

Despite their separate contributions, hip-hop and electronic music have a significant impact on remix culture. New and hybrid forms of music have been produced as a result of the two genres' convergence and cross-pollination.

For example, hip-hop and electronic music elements are combined in genres like trip-hop and drum and bass, which frequently use sampling and looping techniques from both. This cross-pollination has further blurred the lines between genres and fostered a culture of creative reuse.

The Impact on Remix Culture

The impact of hip-hop and electronic music on remix culture can be seen in various aspects:

Both genres have been at the forefront of new techniques like digital manipulation, looping, and sampling, which are now indispensable tools for remixers in a variety of fields.
Traditional ideas of authorship have been questioned by both genres, which has promoted a creative reuse culture in which creators are urged to expand on the work of others.
Genre blurring: Both genres have contributed to the development of new and hybrid musical forms by obfuscating the distinctions between them.
democratizing the creation of music: People can now make and share their music with the world thanks to the accessibility and affordability of digital tools.

Hip-hop and electronic music have played a transformative role in shaping remix culture. By pioneering new techniques, challenging traditional notions of authorship, and fostering a culture of creative re-use, these genres have paved the way for new forms of musical expression. Their influence can be seen not only in music but also in other creative disciplines, demonstrating the power of remix culture to drive innovation and creativity.

4.3 Examples of Famous Remixes and Their Cultural Influence

Since iconic remixes have shaped popular culture and influenced musical trends, music remixing has grown from a specialized activity to a widespread phenomenon. This essay will examine particular case studies of well-known remixes, examining their inventive methods, cultural influence, and enduring legacy.

Grandmaster Flash and the Furious Five's "The Message"

Despite not being a remix in the traditional sense, this 1982 song is regarded as a hip-hop classic and a forerunner of sampling culture. Numerous hip-hop artists were influenced by the song's groundbreaking use of synthesizers, drum machines, and socially conscious lyrics, which also helped to shape the genre's future.

"Planet Rock" (The Soulsonic Force & Africa Bambaataa)

Hip-hop and electronic music were combined in this 1982 song, which also featured Kraftwerk's ***"Trans-Europe Express"*** and ***"Numbers."*** The outcome was a revolutionary sound that shaped the evolution of other electronic music genres, including electro-funk.

"Paid in Full (Seven Minutes of Madness—The Coldcut Remix)" (Rakim & Eric B.)

The British duo Coldcut turned Eric B. & Rakim's hip-hop classic into a more dance-oriented song with this 1987 remix. The remix's creative use of looping and sampling contributed to the technique's rise in popularity and had an impact on the evolution of house music and other electronic genres.

New Order's "Blue Monday"

This 1983 song is noteworthy for its many remixes and re-edits, even though it isn't a remix in the conventional sense. With its lengthy instrumental passages and avant-garde production methods, the song's popular 12-inch version contributed to the format's popularity and shaped the evolution of dance music culture.

Fifth, "I Feel Love" by Donna Summer

This Giorgio Moroder-produced song from 1977 is regarded as a groundbreaking piece of electronic dance music. The song's driving beat and inventive use of synthesizers impacted the growth of techno, house music, and other electronic genres.

Grandmaster Flash's "The Adventures of Grandmaster Flash on the Wheels of Steel"

This 1981 track is a landmark example of turntablism, a technique that involves using turntables as musical instruments. Hip-hop DJing and remix culture developed as a result of Grandmaster Flash's inventive use of scratching, cutting, and mixing techniques.

"Nannacay" (Technotronic)

With its catchy vocals and infectious beat, this 1989 song became a worldwide hit and contributed to the rise in popularity of house music. Numerous re-edits and remixes of the song strengthened its hold on dance music culture.

"U Can't Touch This" (MC Hammer)

This 1990 track, with its prominent sample of Rick James' ***"Super Freak,"*** became a pop culture phenomenon. The song's success helped to popularize sampling in mainstream music and influenced the development of pop-rap.

"Around the World" (Daft Punk)

This 1997 track, with its repetitive vocal sample and hypnotic beat, became a defining work in house music. The song's music video, directed by Michel Gondry, further cemented its cultural impact.

"Ray of Light" (Madonna)

This 1998 track, produced by William Orbit, fused electronic music with pop and world music influences. The song's innovative production and its accompanying music video, directed by Jonas Åkerlund, helped to push the boundaries of pop music and visual culture.

These case studies demonstrate the diverse and far-reaching impact of music remixing. Remixes have shaped popular culture and influenced musical trends by challenging conventional ideas of authorship and inventing new techniques. It will be fascinating to observe how remixing continues to change the music industry as technology advances.

4.4 Mashups' Ascent and Importance in Remixing Classic Works

From straightforward sampling to intricate mashups, the craft of remixing music has transformed how we produce, listen to, and enjoy music. The development of music remixing will be examined in this essay, from the earliest sampling methods to the emergence of remixups and other modern remix formats.

The Basis of Remix Culture: Sampling

A key component of contemporary music is sampling, which is the act of taking a section of an already-recorded song and using it in a new composition. Artists have blended genres and eras by using samples to create new sonic landscapes in everything from hip-hop to electronic music.

Prior to the digital era, sampling was a time-consuming and costly procedure that frequently required physically cutting and splicing magnetic tape. However, the process became much more accessible with the introduction of computer software and digital samplers. Sounds from any source could now be readily sampled, altered, and incorporated into music by artists.

Both the creation and consumption of music have been altered by sampling. Nowadays, listeners are used to hearing well-known sounds in unfamiliar settings, which blurs the distinctions between genres and fosters intertextuality.

Looping: Producing Repeating Textures and Rhythms

In contemporary music, looping—the act of repeating a segment of audio—has also gained popularity. Artists can produce hypnotic and engrossing soundscapes by producing repetitive rhythms and textures.

Tape loops, which were made by physically joining the ends of a piece of magnetic tape, were the first method of looping. But as digital technology advanced, looping became much more accurate and adaptable. It was now simple for artists to construct loops of any length, adjust their pitch and tempo, and layer them to produce intricate rhythmic patterns.

Hip-hop and electronic music are just two of the genres that have been greatly influenced by looping. It has allowed musicians to push the limits of musical expression by producing complex rhythmic patterns and mesmerizing soundscapes.

Digital Manipulation: Creating Unprecedented Sound Changes

Additionally, artists can now manipulate sound in previously unheard-of ways thanks to digital technology. Artists can now precisely adjust the pitch, tempo, timbre, and spatial properties of sound thanks to the development of digital audio workstations (DAWs) and specialized software.

Through the use of digital manipulation techniques, artists are now able to produce sounds that were previously unattainable.

Digital manipulation has evolved into a vital tool for contemporary music production, ranging from minor adjustments to drastic changes.

Mashups' Ascent: Merging Genres and Time Periods

Mashups are a more recent type of remixing in which two or more songs' elements are combined to create a new song. This technique, which combines genres and produces surprising juxtapositions, was made popular by digital audio editing software and has since become a mainstay of remix culture.

In a mashup, the vocals of one song are frequently combined with the instrumental track of another to create a novel and frequently unexpected combination. Artists have been able to produce original and inventive songs that combine various genres and historical periods thanks to this technique.

Music Genres Affected

Digital manipulation, mashups, looping, and sampling have all had a significant influence on different musical genres. For example, sampling has played a significant role in hip-hop, where musicians use samples from a variety of sources to produce original beats and rhythms. These methods have also changed electronic music, with musicians creating intricate and engrossing soundscapes with loops and digital manipulation.

Artists frequently combine elements from various styles to create new and hybrid forms of music, further blurring the boundaries between genres. A rich and varied musical landscape where creativity and experimentation are highly regarded has resulted from the cross-pollination of genres.

Music Production's Democratization

The introduction of digital technologies has altered not only who can create music but also how it is made. Digital tools' accessibility and affordability have democratized music production, enabling anyone to compose and perform music.

Artists are no longer limited to costly studios; they can now produce music of a high caliber from the comfort of their own homes. More people than ever before are able to express themselves through music as a result of this democratization, which has sparked an explosion in creativity.

From sampling to mashups, the development of music remixing has changed the musical landscape and enabled musicians to produce fresh, avant-garde sounds. These methods have altered both the production and consumption of music, obfuscating genre boundaries and

fostering a rich and varied musical environment.

The democratization of music production has also had a significant effect, enabling people to share their works with the world and express themselves through music. It will be fascinating to observe how these methods continue to influence music in the future as technology develops.

4.5 The Impact of Remixing on the Creation of Modern Music

Once a specialized technique, remixing has grown to be an essential component of modern music production, impacting many genres and changing how music is produced, listened to, and valued. The significant influence of remixing on modern music production will be examined in this essay, along with its methods, genre-influencing effects, and contribution to the development of the present musical landscape.

Methods of Remixing: Digital Manipulation, Looping, and Sampling

Several fundamental techniques that are now indispensable tools for modern music producers are at the core of remixing:

Sampling is the process of using a section of an already-recorded song to create a new composition. From brief drum breaks to catchy phrases or vocal lines, sampling can serve as a basis for new songs or introduce a well-known element into an unfamiliar setting.

By repeating a segment of audio, the looping technique produces a melodic or rhythmic motif that can serve as the basis for a track or as a recurrent element in a song.

Digital manipulation: This includes a broad range of methods that modify the timbre, pitch, tempo, and spatial properties of sound using digital tools. The limits of sonic potential can be pushed through the use of digital manipulation to produce subtle improvements or drastic changes.

The Impact on Genres: Electronic Music, Hip-Hop, and Other

Many musical genres have been significantly impacted by remixing, but hip-hop and electronic music have been especially significant.

Hip-hop: Since the genre's inception, sampling has played a significant role, with artists utilizing samples from a variety of sources to produce original beats and rhythms. Numerous classic hip-hop songs that are based on samples from jazz, funk, soul, and other genres have been produced as a result of this practice.

Electronic music: Remixing techniques have also changed electronic music, with musicians creating intricate and engrossing soundscapes with loops and digital manipulation. Remixing has a big impact on genres like house, techno, and drum and bass, as musicians frequently make remixes of their own or other people's songs.

Remixing has impacted pop, rock, and even country music in addition to hip-hop and electronic music. Nowadays, sampling, looping, and digital manipulation are being used by musicians from a variety of genres to produce fresh and inventive sounds.

The Influence of Remixing on the Development of the Present Musical Scene

Both the creation and consumption of music have been impacted by remixing. Listeners are now used to hearing remixes of their favorite songs, and with the growth of digital platforms and streaming services, they frequently come across new versions that present an original viewpoint.

The distinctions between genres have also become less clear as a result of remixing, as musicians frequently combine aspects of various styles to produce original, hybrid music. A rich and varied musical landscape where creativity and experimentation are highly regarded has resulted from the cross-pollination of genres.

Remixing has also made music production more accessible by enabling anyone to compose and release their music. Anyone can now produce remixes of professional quality from the comfort of their own home thanks to the accessibility and affordability of digital tools.

Remixing is now a crucial component of modern music production, impacting many genres and changing how we make, listen to, and enjoy music. Remixing techniques ranging from looping and sampling to digital manipulation and mashups have blurred the boundaries between genres and created new sonic possibilities. It will be fascinating to observe how remixing continues to influence music as technology advances.

Chapter 5:

Visual Culture Remixed: From Fan Art to Memes

Visual culture is continuously being remixed, reinterpreted, and reshared in the current digital era. Remixing has become a fundamental aspect of how we produce, consume, and engage with visual content, from fan art to memes. The various types of visual remixing will be discussed in this essay, along with their cultural significance and effects on the media landscape as a whole.

Fan Art: Honoring Originality and Enthusiasm

As a type of visual remixing, fan art entails producing original artwork inspired by well-known figures, tales, or fictional worlds. Through this practice, fans can connect with other fans who share their interests, express their creativity, and interact more deeply with their favorite media.

Traditional drawings and paintings, digital illustrations, sculptures, and even cosplay are just a few examples of the various forms of fan art. It is present in a variety of online communities, including social media groups, online forums, and fan art websites.

Fan art has grown to be a significant aspect of fandom culture, giving fans a platform to express their passion for their preferred media and produce original interpretations. Additionally, it has developed into a platform for fans to interact with one another and exchange ideas and enthusiasm.

Memes: An Internet Age Language

Another type of visual remixing, memes, have proliferated as a means of cultural expression and online communication. Adapting and reinterpreting preexisting images or phrases to produce fresh, frequently humorous meanings is a common practice in memes.

As they are shared and reinterpreted by various users, memes change and evolve as they quickly spread throughout the internet. They are now an effective means of communicating thoughts, feelings, and cultural criticism.

Additionally, memes have grown to be a significant component of online culture, fostering a common language and set of references that bridge cultural and ethnic divides. They have also evolved into a means of interaction with current affairs, frequently utilizing satire and comedy to make remarks about social and political matters.

The Effect on Visual Culture

Visual culture has been profoundly impacted by the rise of fan art and memes. These remixing techniques have made it possible for anyone to produce and distribute their own visual content, democratizing creativity. Additionally, they have made it harder to distinguish between high and low culture, as memes and fan art frequently take inspiration from both.

Additionally, conventional ideas of authorship and originality have been called into question by fan art and memes. The conventional idea of the lone author is called into question in a culture of remix, where works are frequently produced by combining and reinterpreting preexisting content.

In all of its manifestations, visual remixing has become a vital aspect of modern culture. These practices have changed how we produce, consume, and engage with visual content, from fan art to memes. They have blurred the boundaries between genres and styles, democratized creativity, and questioned conventional ideas of authorship. It will be fascinating to observe how visual remixing continues to influence visual culture as technology advances.

5.1 Analyzing Remixing's Function in Visual Culture

Remixing has become a common practice in today's visually driven world, influencing the way we produce, watch, and engage with images and videos. Remixing has a big influence on visual culture, from memes and fan art to political propaganda and advertising. The various ways that remixing appears in the visual world will be discussed in this essay, along with how it affects communication, creativity, and cultural discourse.

Remixing as a Creative Expression Method

In visual culture, remixing frequently functions as a means of artistic expression, enabling creators to reimagine preexisting pieces, incorporate their own distinct viewpoints, and produce fresh and inventive works.

This can appear in a number of ways:

Fan art is the process of producing original artwork based on well-known figures, tales, or fictional settings from popular culture. Through this practice, fans can connect with other fans who share their interests, express their creativity, and interact more deeply with their favorite media.

Collage and photomontage: These methods combine and alter pre-existing images or other visual materials to produce fresh, frequently fantastical compositions. They can be used to convey artistic ideas, social criticism, or personal experiences.

Video editing and mashups: These techniques entail modifying and fusing pre-existing video content to produce fresh interpretations or stories. They can be used to tell original stories, provide different viewpoints on already-existing media, or produce humorous or satirical content.

Remixing as a Communication Tool

In visual culture, remixing is also a potent means of communication that enables people to convey thoughts, feelings, and cultural commentary.

This can appear in a number of ways:

Memes: Memes have become a common online communication and cultural expression tool, frequently involving the modification and reinterpretation of preexisting images or phrases. As they are shared and reinterpreted by various users, they quickly spread throughout the internet and change and evolve.

Propaganda and advertising: To produce visually appealing and compelling messages, remixing techniques are frequently employed in these fields. This may entail influencing public opinion through satire and comedy, image manipulation, or emotional appeals.

Commentary on social and political issues: Remixing can be used to make strong statements about these topics. Through the recontextualization of preexisting images or the creation of new ones that utilize well-known visual motifs, artists and activists can increase awareness, question accepted wisdom, and encourage social change.

The Development of Visual Culture and Remixing

The development of visual culture has been greatly aided by remixing, which has challenged conventional ideas of authorship, originality, and copyright. The conventional idea of the lone author is called into question in a culture of remix, where works are frequently produced by combining and reinterpreting preexisting content.

Remixing has also made it harder to distinguish between high and low culture, as memes and fan art frequently take inspiration from both. Additionally, it has made creativity more accessible by enabling anyone to produce and distribute original visual content.

Remixing has become a fundamental aspect of modern visual culture, influencing the way we produce, view, and engage with pictures and videos. It has blurred the boundaries between genres and styles, democratized creativity, and questioned conventional ideas of authorship. It will be fascinating to observe how remixing continues to influence visual culture as technology advances.

5.2 The phenomenon of fan art, fan fiction, and other forms of fan-created content.

Fan-generated content has proliferated in the digital age, encompassing cosplay, video edits, fan art, and fan fiction, among other forms. This phenomenon is a reflection of a profound engagement with popular culture, where fans actively participate in the transformation and expansion of the worlds they love, going beyond passive consumption. The various types of fan-generated content will be discussed in this essay, along with their cultural significance, motivations, and effects on the media landscape.

Fan Art: Fandom's Visual Expressions

A vast variety of visual works influenced by current media, such as movies, TV series, video games, books, comics, and music, are referred to as fan art. From conventional paintings and drawings to digital illustrations, sculptures, graphic designs, and even photo manipulations, it can take many different forms.

For both fans and creators, fan art fulfills a number of functions:

Expression of creativity: It gives fans a platform to showcase their artistic abilities and interpretations of their favorite characters and settings.
Emotional connection: By examining themes, relationships, and characters that speak to them, it enables fans to engage with the source material on a deeper emotional level.

Community building: By giving fans a forum for sharing, talking about, and enjoying their common interests, it helps them feel more connected to one another.

Alternative interpretations: In order to provide new viewpoints and increase the scope of the narrative, fan art frequently investigates alternate plotlines, character relationships (shipping), or interpretations of events that deviate from the official canon.

Fan Fiction: Growing Worlds of Storytelling

Writing stories based on pre-existing fictional universes is known as fan fiction, and it is the literary equivalent of fan art. These tales, which cover a variety of subjects, genres, and viewpoints, can be as short as vignettes or as long as novels.

Fan fiction, like fan art, has multiple uses:

Creative writing practice: It gives aspiring authors a place to polish their craft and try out various writing philosophies, and get input from other readers.

Wish fulfillment and "what ifs" exploration: It enables fans to investigate relationships or situations not found in the original source material, satisfying their own desires or investigating different options.

Closing narrative gaps: It can provide a deeper and more comprehensive understanding of the fictional world by elaborating on plots or character backstories that are left unfinished in the original work.

Contesting canonical narratives: By presenting alternate viewpoints or examining marginalized characters, fan fiction has the power to contest or subvert conventional narratives.

Additional Types of Content Produced by Fans:

Other types of fan-generated content have surfaced in addition to fan fiction and fan art, illustrating the variety of ways in which fans interact with popular culture:

Video edits and anime music videos, or AMVs, are the process of reworking preexisting video footage—often set to music—to produce fresh interpretations or stories.

Cosplay is the practice of making and donning costumes inspired by fictional characters. Cosplayers frequently attend conventions and events to display their creations.

Fan games and mods are the process of making original video games or altering pre-existing ones, frequently by adding characters, plots, or other media components.

Vlogs and podcasts: Fans produce video blogs and podcasts to talk about and critique their favorite media, express their thoughts, and interact with other fans.

The Effect on the Media Environment:

Traditional ideas of authorship, copyright, and the relationship between creators and consumers have all been challenged by the rise of fan-created content, which has had a profound effect on the media landscape.

Blurring the boundaries between creator and consumer: As fans actively participate in the production and distribution of media, fan-generated content blurs the boundaries between creator and consumer.

Putting copyright and fair use to the test: Using copyrighted content in fan-made content presents difficult legal issues regarding both fair use and copyright infringement.

Commercial media influence: Some commercial media producers have started incorporating fan concepts or characters into official works as a result of the popularity of fan-generated content. Online communities have grown as a result of fan-generated content, allowing fans to interact, exchange their work, and have conversations about their common interests.

A notable change in the dynamic between media and its audience can be seen in the emergence of fan art, fan fiction, and other fan-generated content. Fans are now active contributors who change and broaden the worlds they adore rather than merely being passive consumers. Traditional ideas of authorship, copyright, and the audience's role have all been challenged by this creative engagement, which has had a significant impact on the media landscape.

5.3 The Development of Internet Memes and Their Contribution to the Spread of Culture

An essential component of online communication and cultural expression are internet memes, the viral sensations of the digital age. As they are shared and reinterpreted by various users, they quickly spread throughout the internet and change and evolve. The phenomenon of internet memes will be examined in this essay, along with its traits, function in the spread of culture, and effects on the media landscape at large.

The attributes of online memes

Typical characteristics of internet memes include their:

Replicability: Memes spread quickly over the internet because they are simple to copy, edit, and distribute.

Variability: As memes are shared, they frequently change and adapt, with various users contributing their own unique twist.

Humor: A lot of memes use irony, satire, or comedy to get their point across, which makes them interesting and viral.

Relatability: A large audience can relate to memes because they frequently draw on common experiences, feelings, or cultural allusions.

The Use of Memes in Cultural Transmission

As a means of disseminating concepts, ideals, and cultural allusions, memes are important in the transmission of culture.

They are useful for:

Communicate shared emotions and experiences: Memes frequently depict universal emotions or experiences, enabling people to relate to others who have similar sentiments.

Social and political commentary: Memes can be used to share thoughts or criticisms about social and political issues, frequently utilizing satire or comedy to get their point across.

Spread inside jokes and cultural references: Memes frequently make reference to particular occasions, fashions, or cultural phenomena, which gives people who are familiar with them a common vocabulary and set of references.

Create a sense of community and belonging: By bringing people together who have similar hobbies or life experiences, memes can foster a sense of belonging and a common identity.

The Effect on the Media Environment

Traditional ideas of authorship, originality, and copyright have been called into question by the emergence of internet memes, which has had a profound effect on the media landscape.

Memes are frequently made and disseminated by regular internet users, which makes it difficult to distinguish between creators and consumers.
Copyright infringement and fair use are complicated legal issues that are brought up by the use of copyrighted content in memes.
Commercial media influence: Memes are now a source of inspiration for marketers and advertisers, who frequently utilize them to develop viral advertising campaigns.
Creating online discourse: Memes have grown to be a crucial component of online discourse, influencing how people engage and communicate with one another online.

Internet memes have grown to be a significant cultural force that shapes our interactions with the outside world, our communication, and our self-expression. They have blurred the boundaries between high and low culture, democratized creativity and questioned conventional ideas of authorship. It will be fascinating to observe how memes continue to influence communication and cultural expression as technology develops.

5.4 The Application of Remixing in Marketing, Propaganda, and Advertising

Remixing—the act of taking preexisting elements and rearranging them—has grown in popularity as a marketing, propaganda, and advertising tactic. Through the recontextualization of well-known images, sounds, and concepts, these domains are able to produce compelling and captivating messages. The numerous applications of remixing in these settings will be discussed in this essay, along with how it affects public opinion and consumer behavior.

In marketing and advertising, remixing

Remixing is frequently used in marketing and advertising to develop campaigns that connect with target consumers.

This may include:

Popular songs, movie sequences, and other cultural allusions are frequently sampled in advertisements to establish a feeling of familiarity and connection with viewers.

Re-creating classic advertisements: To appeal to brand recognition and nostalgia, advertisers occasionally re-create classic advertisements with a contemporary twist.

User-generated content: To engage customers as active participants in the marketing process, marketers frequently encourage users to produce original content that highlights their brands or products.

Using Remixes in Advertising

Remixing techniques are also employed in propaganda, which is the dissemination of information to support a specific cause or ideology.

This may include:

Images and videos are frequently manipulated by propaganda in order to skew the facts or elicit a particular emotional reaction.
Historical events can be recontextualized by propaganda in order to bolster a specific narrative or to malign a different point of view.
Using well-known symbols and phrases: In order to foster a sense of solidarity and to evoke strong feelings in people, propaganda frequently makes use of well-known symbols and phrases.

Remixing's Effect on Public Opinion and Consumer Behavior

Remixing can significantly influence public opinion and consumer behavior. Advertisers and propagandists can craft persuasive and captivating messages by rearranging well-known components. By encouraging people to identify with a specific brand or ideology, remixing can also be used to foster a sense of community and belonging.

But there are also moral questions about the use of remixing in marketing, propaganda, and advertising. Critics contend that it can be used to spread damaging stereotypes, twist the facts, or control people's emotions.

Remixing has become a fundamental aspect of modern culture, impacting everything from music and art to propaganda and advertising. We can become more informed citizens and critical media consumers by comprehending how remixing is used in these situations.

5.5 Digital Manipulation's Effect on Photography and Video

The emergence of digital manipulation in the field of visual media has brought about a paradigm shift, significantly altering the field of photography and video. Now that they are not limited by the limitations of conventional methods, artists have unheard-of control over their creations, pushing the limits of imagination and realism. The many facets of digital manipulation will be examined in this essay, including how it affects ethical issues, artistic expression, and the changing dynamic between representation and reality.

Improved Artistic Expression and Creative Control

By giving people easily accessible tools to improve, modify, and reimagine their visual content, digital manipulation has democratized the creative process. From intricate composing and special effects to color correction and retouching, photographers and videographers can now perfect every element of their work. A surge in artistic experimentation has resulted from this newfound control, creating previously unattainable surreal imagery, fantastical worlds, and compelling visual narratives.

The Distinguishing Between Representation and Reality

The distinction between representation and reality has become more hazy due to the ease with which digital tools can edit photos and videos. This has sparked worries about the possibility of deceit and manipulation, especially in industries where authenticity and accuracy are crucial, like journalism and advertising. Our understanding of truth and objectivity in visual media has been called into question by the ability to easily erase flaws, change the shape of bodies, and create whole scenes.

The Responsibility of Creators and Ethical Considerations

Because of the power of digital manipulation, it is important to use these tools in an ethical and open manner. The possible effects of their work must be considered by creators, who must refrain from reinforcing negative stereotypes, misrepresenting the truth, and raising irrational expectations. Keeping audiences' trust and transparency can be maintained by being open about the use of digital manipulation.

Visual Storytelling's Development

Visual storytelling has been transformed by digital manipulation, allowing filmmakers and videographers to produce engrossing and immersive stories. Creators can now bring their most imaginative ideas to life, take viewers to fantastical worlds, and portray historical events with breathtaking realism thanks to special effects, computer-generated imagery, and composing techniques.

The Democratization of Photography and Filmmaking

Digital cameras, editing software, and online platforms have made photography and filmmaking more accessible, enabling anyone to tell their story and share it with the world. Independent filmmaking, web series, and user-generated content have all increased as a result, adding to the variety of voices and viewpoints in visual media.

The Effect on Marketing and Advertising

Digital manipulation is now a crucial component of marketing and advertising, enabling businesses to develop eye-catching campaigns that draw in customers and advertise their goods and services. However, the potential for consumers to be misled and have irrational expectations has also prompted ethical concerns regarding the use of digital manipulation in these fields.

Social Media's Influence on Visual Culture

With users having easy access to editing tools, filters, and face-tuning applications, social media platforms have turned into a haven for digital manipulation. This has caused curated online personas to proliferate, in which people showcase idealized versions of themselves, frequently making it difficult to distinguish fact from fiction.

Digital Manipulation's Future

The potential for digital manipulation is only going to grow as technology develops further. Virtual reality, artificial intelligence, and machine learning have the potential to further transform the field by obfuscating the distinction between simulation and reality and upending our preconceived notions about visual media.

Digital manipulation has permanently changed the photography and video industries by giving artists previously unheard-of control and creative potential. But with this authority also comes the duty to employ these instruments in a morally and openly responsible manner. In order to navigate the constantly shifting relationship between reality and representation in visual media, it is imperative that we cultivate a critical understanding of digital manipulation as technology advances.

Chapter 6:

Narrative Remixed: Retellings, Adaptations, and Transmedia Storytelling

Storytelling has always been a dynamic art form, with stories changing and developing over time and between cultures. Remixing has become a crucial component of storytelling in today's media environment, which has fueled the growth of transmedia storytelling, adaptations, and retellings. These interrelated phenomena will be examined in this essay, along with their traits, cultural significance, and effects on the media landscape as a whole.

Retellings: Reimagining Traditional Stories

Retellings entail going over old tales, myths, or historical occurrences again while providing fresh viewpoints or interpretations. They frequently explore different themes, characters, or settings and can range from faithful adaptations to radical reinterpretations.

Retellings accomplish a number of goals:

Making stories accessible to new audiences: Retellings of classic stories can make them more interesting and relevant for modern audiences by changing the language, settings, or themes.

Examining various points of view: Retellings can present different perspectives on well-known tales, questioning accepted interpretations or providing voice to underrepresented characters.

Commenting on current events: Retellings of classic tales can serve as a prism through which to view current events in politics, society, or culture.

Changes: Changing Narratives in Various Media

Transforming stories from one medium to another, like from a comic book to a stage play, a video game to a television show, or a book to a movie, is known as adaptation. As the story is modified to conform to the rules and limitations of the new medium, this process frequently entails substantial changes to the narrative.

Adaptations have multiple uses:

Increasing a story's audience: By converting a story to a different format, authors can connect with more people who might not have heard of the original work.

Investigating new creative possibilities: Adapting a story to a new medium can give storytellers the chance to try out new visual styles or storytelling approaches.

Creating new revenue streams: Adaptations can be a profitable method for artists to make money off of their creations, bringing in new money from various media.

Transmedia Storytelling: Using Various Platforms to Tell Stories

Telling a single story across several media platforms—including movies, TV series, video games, books, comics, and social media—is known as transmedia storytelling. Every platform adds a distinct element to the overall story, making the audience's experience more captivating and immersive.

Transmedia narrative has multiple uses:

Providing a more immersive and captivating experience: By presenting a story on several platforms, producers can give viewers a more immersive and captivating experience that enables them to examine the story from various angles and in a variety of media formats.

Increasing a story's audience: By utilizing a variety of platforms, producers can connect with a larger audience that might have varying media preferences.

Creating a closer bond with the audience: Through interaction with the story on various platforms, viewers can become more invested in the characters, the setting, and the story as a whole.

The Effect on the Media Environment

Traditional ideas of authorship, originality, and the relationship between creators and audiences have all been challenged by the rise of retellings, adaptations, and transmedia storytelling.

Blurring the boundaries between creator and consumer: In transmedia storytelling, viewers frequently take an active role in the story, contributing their own material or directing its course.

Difficult legal issues regarding copyright infringement and fair use are brought up by the use of copyrighted content in retellings and adaptations.

In the entertainment industry, transmedia storytelling has sparked the creation of new business models as producers and studios look for innovative ways to make money off of their work on various platforms.

In conclusion

Transmedia storytelling, adaptations, and retellings have all become essential components of modern media culture, influencing how people hear and interact with stories. They have blurred the boundaries between genres and styles, democratized creativity, and questioned conventional ideas of authorship. It will be interesting to observe how these remixing techniques continue to influence storytelling in the future as technology develops.

6.1 Examining the Idea of Story Remixing in Film, Literature, and Other Media

The idea of remixing has gained popularity in today's media-rich society, reaching beyond the visual and musical arts to include storytelling. Reconfiguring preexisting stories, characters, or themes to produce new works is known as narrative remixing. This practice appears in a variety of media, including video games, literature, movies, and transmedia projects. The idea of narrative remixing will be examined in this essay, along with its various manifestations, cultural significance, and effects on the media landscape as a whole.

Types of Story Remixing

A vast array of artistic disciplines are included in narrative remixing, each with distinctive qualities of its own:

Retellings: Retellings entail going over old tales, myths, or historical occurrences again while providing fresh viewpoints or interpretations. They frequently explore different themes, characters, or settings and can range from faithful adaptations to radical reinterpretations.

The process of converting stories from one medium to another, like from a comic book to a stage play, a video game to a television show, or a book to a movie, is known as adaptation. As the story is modified to conform to the rules and limitations of the new medium, this process frequently entails substantial changes to the narrative.

Pastiche is the imitation of a specific author, artist, or genre; it frequently combines elements from various sources to produce a new work that is both familiar and unique.

Parody is the act of mimicking a work for humorous effect, frequently exaggerating or changing certain aspects of it to produce satire or humor.

Fan fiction is the creation of stories based on pre-existing fictional worlds, frequently examining different plotlines, character interactions, or interpretations of events that deviate from the accepted canon.

Telling a single story across several media platforms, including movies, TV series, video games, books, comics, and social media, is known as transmedia storytelling. Every platform adds a distinct element to the overall story, making the audience's experience more captivating and immersive.

Reasons for Remixing Narratives

There are several reasons why narrative remixing is done, such as:

Creative expression: Remixing gives artists a platform to explore new creative possibilities or to convey their own interpretations of stories that already exist.

Cultural commentary: Using humor or satire to make a point, remixing can be used to comment on social, political, or cultural issues.

Engagement of the audience: By allowing viewers to take part in the telling or interpretation of a story, remixing can be a means to interact with them more deeply.

Commercial considerations: Remixing can help artists make money off of their creations by creating new revenue streams through spin-offs or adaptations.

Influence on the Media Environment

Traditional ideas of authorship, originality, and the relationship between creators and audiences have all been challenged by the emergence of narrative remixing, which has had a profound effect on the media landscape.

The distinction between creator and consumer is blurred in remix culture, as audiences frequently take an active role in the production and distribution of media.

Difficult legal issues regarding copyright infringement and fair use are brought up by the use of copyrighted content in narrative remixing.

New business models are being developed for the entertainment industry as a result of narrative remixing with producers and studios looking into novel ways to make money off of their work on various platforms.

The way stories are told and experienced has been shaped by narrative remixing, which has become a fundamental aspect of modern media culture. It has blurred the boundaries between genres and styles, democratized creativity, and questioned conventional ideas of authorship. It will be fascinating to observe how narrative remixing continues to influence storytelling in the future as technology develops.

6.2 The Function of Sequels, Remakes, and Adaptations in Continuing Current Storylines

Adaptations, remakes, and sequels are essential to extending existing narratives and giving cherished characters and worlds new life in the vast and constantly growing world of storytelling. These kinds of imaginative reuse present special chances to investigate various viewpoints, go over well-known subjects again, and build on folklore. The unique qualities of each form will be explored in this essay, along with their motivations, effects on the media landscape, and difficulties in meeting the needs of both audiences and creators.

Adaptations: Overcoming the Divide In between media

Translating a story from one medium to another, like from a comic book to a video game, a play to a musical, or a book to a movie, is known as adaptation. The story must frequently be significantly altered during this process in order to conform to the rules and limitations of the new medium.

Adaptations accomplish a number of important goals:

Reaching a larger audience: Storytellers can reach a larger audience who might not be familiar with the original work by adapting their work to a new medium.

Investigating new creative possibilities: Adapting a story to a new medium can give storytellers the chance to try out new visual styles or storytelling approaches.

Creating new revenue streams: Adaptations can be a profitable method for artists to make money off of their creations, bringing in new money from various media.

Remakes: Retelling Tales for Upcoming Generations

In a remake, a story that has previously been told in the same medium is revisited; for example, a television series may be rebooted or a movie may be remade as another movie. A common goal of remakes is to bring the story up to date for a modern audience by introducing new viewpoints, cultural trends, or technological advancements.

Remakes accomplish a number of important goals:

Reaching new audiences: Younger generations who might not be familiar with the original versions of classic stories can be introduced to them through remakes.

Stories can be updated for modern audiences through remakes to take into account new social issues, values, or attitudes.

Investigating fresh interpretations: Remakes can provide fresh takes on well-known tales, examining various themes or the motivations of the characters.

Sequels: Extending the Narrative Past the Initial Conclusion

Sequels carry on a work's plot, frequently concentrating on the same characters or developing the preexisting world. Sequels can delve deeper into the original work's lore, introduce new characters, or explore new storylines.

Sequels have multiple important uses:

Sequels can give fans more of what they enjoy, such as revisiting familiar worlds or carrying on the stories of cherished characters.
Investigating fresh creative possibilities: Sequels can give producers the opportunity to experiment with novel plotlines or character arcs.
Creating new revenue streams: By building on the established popularity of the original work, sequels can be a profitable way for creators to make money off of their creations.

The Effect on the Media Environment

The media landscape has been significantly impacted by the rise of adaptations, remakes, and sequels, which have put traditional ideas of authorship, originality, and the relationship between creators and audiences to the test.

In a world where stories are continuously being remade, adapted, and sequelized, audiences frequently take an active role in the production and interpretation of narratives, blurring the boundaries between creator and consumer.

Contesting fair use and copyright: Complex legal issues regarding copyright infringement and fair use are brought up by the use of copyrighted content in sequels, remakes, and adaptations.

Developing fresh business plans: The popularity of sequels, remakes, and adaptations has prompted the entertainment industry to develop new business models as producers and studios look for new ways to make money off of their work on various platforms.

The way stories are told and experienced has been shaped by adaptations, remakes, and sequels, which are now essential components of modern media culture. They have blurred the boundaries between genres and styles, democratized creativity, and questioned conventional ideas of authorship. It will be interesting to observe how these remixing techniques continue to influence storytelling in the future as technology develops.

6.3. Transmedia Storytelling's Development and Dependency on Cross-Platform Remixing

Transmedia storytelling is a phenomenon that has emerged in the modern media landscape as storytelling has moved beyond the confines of individual platforms. This strategy entails presenting a single story in a variety of media, including movies, TV series, video games, comic books, books, websites, social media, and even actual events. In order to give the audience a more immersive and captivating experience, transmedia storytelling relies heavily on remixing, modifying, and extending the main plot across these various platforms. The development of transmedia storytelling will be examined in this essay, with particular attention paid to how it depends on remixing methods and how it affects audience participation.

Transmedia Storytelling: A Definition

Adapting a story from one medium to another is only one aspect of transmedia storytelling.

Rather, it entails developing a cohesive story experience that spans several platforms, with each one adding a distinct piece to the whole. With varying degrees of engagement and appeal to distinct audiences, each platform provides a unique way to get started with the story.

Among the essential elements of transmedia storytelling are:

Narrative extension: Every medium adds new viewpoints, plots, or character development to the main narrative.

World-building: Rich and intricate fictional worlds that are explored on various platforms are frequently produced by transmedia projects.

Participation of the audience: Through fan art, fan fiction, online forums, or alternate reality games *(ARGs),* transmedia storytelling frequently invites audience members to participate in the story.

Unified narrative experience: Although every platform provides a different experience, they all work together to create a coherent and comprehensive story.

One of the Fundamentals of Transmedia Storytelling: Remixing

In transmedia storytelling, remixing is essential because it enables creators to modify and extend the story across various platforms.

This may include:

Core narrative elements are modified and reinterpreted for various media formats, such as important characters, plot points, or themes.
Developing new content from preexisting elements: The fictional universe is expanded by developing new stories, characters, or plotlines from the core narrative.
Telling different parts of the story with different media: Various media are used to tell different parts of the story, focusing on different aspects of the narrative or providing different perspectives.

Including user-generated content: The distinction between creator and consumer is frequently blurred when fan art, fan fiction, and other types of user-generated content are integrated into the transmedia experience.

Transmedia Storytelling and Remixing Examples

The following noteworthy instances demonstrate how remixing is used in transmedia storytelling:

Beyond the original movies, the Matrix franchise grew to include animated shorts, video games, comics, and web content, all of which presented unique viewpoints on the Matrix universe.

Alternate reality games (ARGs) and online content were used in the television series Lost to let viewers explore the show's mythology and work through mysteries with the characters.

The MCU, or Marvel Cinematic Universe: This franchise tells a vast story that spans several movies, TV series, and streaming services, with each entry adding to the overall plot.

A vast and interconnected universe has been created by the long-running British science fiction series Doctor Who, which has grown into multiple spin-offs, books, comics, audio dramas, and online content.

Effect on the Engagement of the Audience

The use of remixing in transmedia storytelling has a big effect on audience participation.

Enhanced immersion: Viewers are drawn deeper into the fictional world by interacting with the story on various platforms.

Increased audience participation: Transmedia storytelling frequently makes viewers active participants in the story.

Increased emotional connection: Viewers can strengthen their emotional bond with the characters and the story by examining it from various angles and in a variety of media formats.

Creating online communities: Transmedia projects frequently encourage the development of online communities where viewers can interact, exchange stories, and add to the story.

Transmedia storytelling has revolutionized the media landscape by providing fresh and creative approaches to audience engagement and story telling. In this process, remixing is essential because it enables creators to modify and extend stories across various platforms. The relationship between media and its audience has been redefined by transmedia storytelling, which blurs the boundaries between creator and consumer and promotes audience participation.

6.4 The impact of fan fiction and other forms of participatory culture on narrative remixing.

Fan Fiction and Other Participatory Cultures' Effect on Narrative Remixing

The emergence of participatory culture in the digital age has had a significant impact on how stories are produced, viewed, and re-created. A good illustration of this phenomenon is fan fiction, which, along with other fan-generated content like cosplay, video edits, and fan art, has become a significant influence on narrative remixing. The many facets of participatory culture's influence on narrative remixing will be discussed in this essay, including how it has democratized creativity, questioned conventional ideas of authorship, and encouraged innovative storytelling techniques.

Fan Fiction: Expanding and Reimagining Storyworlds

Writing stories based on pre-existing fictional universes, characters, or plots is known as fan fiction, which is a type of narrative remixing. It enables fans to offer their own interpretations of the original work, investigate alternate scenarios, and delve deeper into character relationships.

Fan fiction has a number of important traits:

Intertextuality: It makes extensive use of pre-existing texts, fostering a conversation between the fan-made and original works.
Participatory authorship: As fans actively participate in the production and distribution of narratives, it questions the conventional idea of the lone author.
Creating a sense of community: It gives fans a forum for exchanging, talking about, and working together on their artistic endeavors.

Additional Types of Narrative Remixing and Participatory Culture

In addition to fan fiction, narrative remixing is facilitated by other types of participatory culture:

Fan art: Visual works that draw inspiration from current media and give fans a platform to showcase their artistic abilities and interpretations.

Editing pre-existing video footage, frequently set to music, to produce new stories or interpretations is known as video editing and anime music videos, or AMVs.

Cosplay: Dressing up as fictional characters and reinterpreting and embodying their identities.

Vlogs and podcasts: Fans produce video blogs and podcasts to talk about and critique their favorite media, express their thoughts, and interact with other fans.

Effect on Remixing Narratives

Narrative remixing has been significantly influenced by participatory culture.

Democratization of creativity: It has removed long-standing barriers to entry in the creative industries by enabling people to produce and disseminate their own versions of preexisting narratives.

Traditional ideas of authorship are being challenged because fans are now actively involved in the production and distribution of stories, obfuscating the distinction between creator and consumer.

The investigation of novel plotlines, character interactions, and interpretations that might not have been covered in the original source material has resulted in the expansion of narrative possibilities.

New storytelling techniques: It has encouraged the creation of new storytelling techniques, like transmedia storytelling, which tells a single story across several media platforms.

Narrative remixing has been transformed by participatory culture, with fan fiction at its forefront. It has encouraged new storytelling techniques, democratized creativity, and questioned conventional ideas of authorship. It will be interesting to observe how participatory culture continues to influence the direction of narrative remixing as new platforms and technological advancements occur.

6.5 Examples from Literature, Video Games, Television, and Film

The idea of remixing has influenced many media, resulting in the production of fresh and inventive works that expand on preexisting themes, characters, and narratives. Let's look at some noteworthy instances of remixing in literature, video games, television, and movies.

Movie:

"O Brother, Where Art Thou?" (2000): Homer's epic poem *"The Odyssey,"* set in the American South during the Great Depression, is retold in this Coen Brothers film. The film adds its own special twists and turns while retaining aspects of the original poem, like the protagonist's sly nature, the journey home, and encounters with mythical creatures.

Amy Heckerling's 1995 teen comedy "Clueless" is a contemporary adaptation of Jane Austen's *"Emma."* Cher Horowitz plays a modern-day

250

Emma Woodhouse in the movie, which sets the story in Beverly Hills in the 1990s.

The 1994 animated Disney picture "The Lion King" is based on William Shakespeare's play **"Hamlet."** In order to regain his rightful position as king, Simba, a lion cub, must exact revenge for the death of his father.

TV:

Steven Moffat and Mark Gatiss created the British television series ***"Sherlock"*** (2010–2017), which is a contemporary adaptation of Sir Arthur Conan Doyle's Sherlock Holmes novels. Martin Freeman plays Dr. John Watson, and Benedict Cumberbatch plays Sherlock Holmes in the series, which takes place in 21st-century London.

Edward Kitsis and Adam Horowitz are the creators of the American television series ***"Once Upon a Time"*** (2011–2018), which retells traditional fairy tales in a modern setting. As Emma Swan learns she is the daughter of Snow

White and Prince Charming follows her as she works to help the fairy tale characters who have been brought to the real world regain their lost memories.

Michael Crichton's 1973 film of the same name served as the inspiration for Jonathan Nolan and Lisa Joy's science fiction television series *"Westworld"* (2016–present). The show investigates the nature of reality, free will, and artificial intelligence.

Video games:

The 2010 fan-made video game *"Super Mario Bros. Crossover"* blends the gameplay of the original *"Super Mario Bros."* with characters from other vintage video games, including Simon Belmont from *"Castlevania,"* Mega Man, and Link from *"The Legend of Zelda."*

From 1999 to the present, the *"Super Smash Bros."* series: Characters from several Nintendo franchises, including Mario, Link, Pikachu, and

Kirby, appear in this crossover fighting game series. Players can battle their favorite characters in the games, resulting in original and frequently comical matchups.

From 2002 to the present, the *"Kingdom Hearts"* series: Characters and settings from the "*Final Fantasy"* video game series are combined with those from Disney animated movies in this action role-playing game series. The games examine light and dark, friendship, and the strength of the heart.

Books:

Jean Rhys' 1966 book *"The Wide Sargasso Sea"* is a feminist and postcolonial reaction to Charlotte Brontë's *"Jane Eyre."* The book explores the past and experiences of Antoinette Cosway, the *"madwoman in the attic"* from Charlotte Brontë's book, and gives her a voice.

Margaret Atwood's novella *"The Penelopiad"* (2005) retells Homer's *"Odyssey"* from the viewpoint of Odysseus's wife, Penelope. The novella examines Penelope's struggles and experiences during Odysseus' protracted absence, providing a feminist interpretation of the epic poem.

Seth Grahame-Smith's 2009 parody book ***"Pride and Prejudice and Zombies"*** blends elements of zombie horror with Jane Austen's ***"Pride and Prejudice."*** The Bennet sisters are recast as zombie slayers in the book, giving the traditional romance a fun and exciting new dimension.

These illustrations show how remixing can be applied in a variety of imaginative ways to produce fresh and captivating works in a range of media. By referencing pre-existing stories, characters, and themes, artists can present new angles, investigate uncharted territory, and meaningfully interact with viewers.

Chapter 7:

Identity Remixed: Self-Presentation in the Digital Age

Because of how we portray ourselves online, our identities have become more complex and fluid in the digital age. Virtual worlds, online communities, and social media platforms give us new ways to express ourselves and enable us to curate and remix our identities in previously unattainable ways. Identity remixing is a phenomenon that will be discussed in this essay along with how we create and portray ourselves online, why we do it, and how it affects our sense of self.

Building an Online Identity: A Curated Self

We have a rare opportunity in the digital sphere to create and display identities that are different from our offline personas. By carefully choosing the data, pictures, and other content we wish to share with the world, we can curate our online personas. By emphasizing our values, interests, and strengths, this curatorial process enables us to produce an idealized or aspirational version of ourselves.

In particular, social media sites have evolved into a platform for self-presentation. We take great care when creating our posts, selecting the ideal words, pictures, and filters to express a specific idea or message. We also practice impression management, which involves keeping an eye on how people see us online and modifying our actions accordingly.

Reasons to Remix Your Identity

Identity remixing is a practice that is driven by a number of factors in the digital age:

Self-expression: We can explore various facets of our identities and establish connections with people who have similar interests thanks to the digital sphere.
Social connection: Online platforms give us the chance to meet people, form bonds with them,

and locate groups that are similar to our interests or values.

Self-discovery: As we explore various facets of our identities and get input from others, the process of creating and presenting ourselves online can result in self-discovery.

Play and experimentation: The digital world offers a secure environment for play and experimentation, enabling us to adopt various personas or identities without fear of repercussions in the real world.

Effects on Our Self-Concept

Identity remixing can have a significant effect on how we perceive ourselves. Curating our online personas can help us become more self-aware as we consider how we want other people to see us.

On the other hand, the continual pressure to project an idealized self online can also result in anxiety, feelings of inadequacy, or a disconnection between our online and offline selves. Aiming for authenticity and balance in our online and offline lives is crucial, as is being aware of the possible effects of identity remixing.

Identity remixing has become a crucial aspect of the digital age, influencing the way we create and display our identities on the internet. It has made self-expression more accessible, questioned established ideas of identity, and made it harder to distinguish between the real and the virtual worlds. It will be fascinating to observe how identity remixing continues to influence how people connect and present themselves as technology advances.

7.1 Analyzing How People in the Digital Age Remix Their Identities

Through online interactions and self-presentation, people in the digital age have access to previously unheard-of possibilities to create and modify their identities. Often called ***"identity remixing,"*** this process entails selecting, modifying, and showcasing various facets of oneself on a variety of digital platforms. This essay will examine the various ways people remix their identities on the internet, looking at the causes, workings, and effects of this practice.

Taking Care of the Digital Self

People carefully curate their digital presence, which is one of the main ways they remix their identities online. People use personal websites, online portfolios, and social media profiles as canvases for self-expression, choosing and showcasing particular facets of themselves.

This curation entails:

Selective sharing: People highlight parts of their lives that they think are important or appealing and decide which updates, images, and information to share.

Customization of profiles: Bios, background photos, and profile pictures are all chosen with care to project a specific image or message.

Content creation and sharing: People further develop their online persona by producing and disseminating content that reflects their values, beliefs, or interests.

Getting Used to Various Online Situations

People frequently modify their online personas to fit various online situations. A person's appearance on social media sites like Instagram or Twitter may be very different from how they present themselves on professional networking sites like LinkedIn.

This modification entails:

Awareness of the audience: People modify their language, tone, and content according to the platform's perceived audience.

Platform conventions: People follow the unique guidelines and standards of each platform, such as sharing visual content on Instagram or using hashtags on Twitter.

Role-playing and persona adoption: People may experiment with various facets of their identities by taking on various roles or personas in various online communities.

Using Online Interactions to Perform Identity

People can act out their identities through online interactions, interacting with others in ways that either support or contradict how they see themselves.

This performance includes:

Communication style: Depending on the situation, people use different communication styles. For example, they may use formal language in a professional setting or informal language in a social one.

Online behavior: A person's entire online persona is influenced by their online activities, such as liking, sharing, and commenting on content.

Self-presentation through avatars and virtual worlds: People can make avatars that represent themselves in online games or virtual worlds, which enables more identity and self-expression experimentation.

Reasons to Remix Your Identity

People remix their identities online for a variety of reasons:

Self-expression and exploration: People can express their uniqueness and investigate various facets of themselves in the digital sphere.

Social connection and belonging: In an effort to feel a sense of community and belonging, people may remix their identities in order to connect with people who have similar values or interests.

Self-enhancement and impression management: People may curate their online personas to project a favorable image to others in an effort to gain social acceptance or boost their self-esteem.

Play and experimentation: The digital world provides a secure environment where people can try out various personas or identities without fear of repercussions in the real world.

Identity Remixing's Effects

Identity remixing can have both beneficial and detrimental effects:

Increased self-awareness and self-discovery: Creating and presenting online personas can bring about an increase in self-awareness and self-discovery.

Enhanced community building and social connection: People can feel more a part of a community and connect with others through online platforms.

Possibility of deceit and misrepresentation: Since people may present exaggerated or idealized versions of themselves, the capacity to curate online personas can also result in deceit or misrepresentation.

Effect on offline identity and self-perception: People's offline identities and self-perception may be impacted by their continuous online identity performance, which may cause a gap between their online and offline selves.

Identity remixing has grown to be a crucial aspect of the digital age, influencing how people perceive and portray themselves. People participate in a dynamic process of self-creation and self-expression by curating, modifying, and performing various facets of themselves online. It is essential to comprehend identity remixing's causes, workings, and effects in order to successfully navigate the digital world's intricacies and build genuine relationships there.

7.2 The role of social media in shaping online identities.

Social media's introduction has fundamentally changed how we create and display our identities. These platforms have evolved into online stages where we manage the challenges of self-representation in the digital age, curate our personas, and interact with others. The mechanisms, driving forces, and effects of social media's complex role in forming online identities will all be covered in this essay.

Identity Formation and Self-Presentation

Social media sites give users the resources they need to create the online persona they want. People meticulously choose and showcase particular facets of themselves through their profiles, posts, and shared content.

This carefully considered self-presentation includes:

Profile Creation: To express a specific message or image, users create profiles with carefully selected bios, background photos, and profile pictures.

Content Sharing: To showcase their experiences, values, and interests, users share a variety of content, such as images, videos, and text updates.

Impression Management: In order to preserve a desired image, users keep an eye on how other people see them online and modify their behavior and content accordingly.

Validation and Social Interaction

Social media sites make it easier to communicate with people and offer chances for online personas to be validated and reinforced.

This social exchange consists of:

Making Connections with Like-Minded People: Users create online communities that support their identities by connecting with people who have similar values, interests, or backgrounds.

Seeking Approval and Validation: In order to get social validation and affirmation for their online identities, users look for likes, comments, and shares on their content.

Social Comparison: People use social media to compare themselves to others, which can affect how they see themselves and how they present themselves online.

Exploration and Experimentation with Identity

People can experiment with various facets of their identities on social media platforms, pursuing new passions, ideals, or personas.

This experiment includes:

Trying on Different Personas: In order to explore different aspects of themselves, users may take on various personas or roles in various online communities.

Testing New Concepts and Beliefs: People may post new concepts or beliefs online in order to see how others respond and to improve their own viewpoints.

Getting Validation and Feedback: Users get input on their online personas from other people, which can affect how they view themselves and how their identities are formed.

The Effect on Mental Health and Self-Esteem

Self-esteem and mental health can be impacted by the carefully constructed online personas in both positive and negative ways. Social media can foster a feeling of community and connection, but it can also result in anxiety, depression, and social comparison.

Benefits: Social media can encourage community development, self-expression, and creativity, all of which have a positive effect on self-esteem.

Negative Effects: Pressure to uphold an idealized online persona, cyberbullying, and social comparison can all have a detrimental effect on mental health.

How Online and Offline Personas Become Confused

The distinction between our online and offline identities is becoming more hazy as social media becomes more and more ingrained in our daily lives. How we view ourselves and interact with others in the real world can be influenced by our online personas.

Online Behaviors Affecting Offline Interactions: Our relationships and social skills can be shaped by the behavior and communication we exhibit online.

Virtual Personas Shaping Self-Perception: Our sense of authenticity and self-perception may be impacted by the disconnection between our online and offline selves caused by the carefully manicured appearance of our online personas.

Social media now plays a crucial role in the way we create, display, and understand who we are. Even though these platforms present previously unheard-of chances for exploration, connection, and self-expression, it is important to consider the possible effects on mental health, self-esteem, and the blurring of online and offline identities. Maintaining a strong sense of self and establishing genuine connections while navigating the constantly changing digital landscape requires striking a healthy balance between our online and offline lives.

7.3 Using Profiles, Avatars, and Other Online Self-Representation Tools

A new era of self-representation has been brought about by the digital age, in which people use a variety of online tools and platforms to create and project their identities. In the digital sphere, avatars, profiles, and other online self-representations have become essential to our interactions, connections, and self-expression. The various ways people use these tools will be examined in this essay, along with the reasons behind, workings of, and consequences of online self-representation.

Digital Embodiment through Avatars

In virtual worlds, online games, and social media platforms, avatars—digital representations of users—act as visual embodiments.

They provide a special chance to investigate various facets of identity, enabling users to:

Construct idealized or aspirational selves: Users are able to create avatars that represent their idealized social standing, personality, or physical attributes.

Try on different personas: Avatars offer a secure environment where users can explore different facets of themselves without fear of repercussions in the real world.

Express individuality and creativity: Users can add distinctive features, apparel, and accessories to their avatars to show off their individuality and creativity.

Profiles Self-Portraits Curated

Online profiles are carefully curated self-portraits that can be found on dating apps, professional networking sites, and social media platforms. In order to portray a specific image or message, users meticulously choose and display data, images, and other content.

This curation entails:

Selective disclosure is when users decide which details of their lives to share, emphasizing those they find interesting or desirable.
Impression management: To preserve a desired image, users keep an eye on how other people view their profiles and modify their content accordingly.
Narrative construction: Through their profiles, users create stories about themselves that influence how other people perceive them and their experiences.

Additional Online Self-Representation Formats

Other online self-representation techniques, in addition to avatars and profiles, aid in the creation of digital identities:

As digital identifiers, usernames and handles frequently represent the interests, character traits, or online personas of users.

Shared content: The images, videos, articles, and status updates that people post online help to define their online persona and represent their values and worldview.

Digital identities are further shaped by users' behavior, tone, and communication style in online interactions.

Digital footprints: Information about a user's online activities, such as their search queries, browsing history, and online purchases, can be used to determine their preferences, interests, and even personality traits.

Reasons for Self-Representation Online

People participate in online self-representation for a number of reasons:

Self-expression and identity exploration: People can express their uniqueness and investigate various facets of themselves in the digital sphere.

Social interaction and community development: Online platforms provide chances to get in touch with people who have similar values or interests, which promotes a feeling of belonging.

Self-enhancement and impression management: People may curate their online persona to project a favorable image to others in an effort to gain social acceptance or boost their self-esteem.

Reaching particular objectives: People may use their online personas to reach particular objectives, like landing a job, expanding their professional network, or finding love.

Consequences of Self-Representation Online

Online self-representation has a number of implications.

Blurring of online and offline identities: The line separating our digital and real-world selves becomes increasingly hazy as our online and offline lives become more integrated.

Effect on mental health and self-esteem: The carefully manicured appearance of one's online self-portrayal can cause anxiety, social comparison, and pressure to uphold a perfect online image.

Privacy issues: Data security and privacy issues are brought up by the online gathering and exchange of personal data.

Effect on interpersonal relationships: Our online and offline interactions with others can be influenced by how we portray ourselves online.

Online self-representation tools such as avatars and profiles have become indispensable for expressing our identities and navigating the digital world. Although these tools present previously unheard-of chances for connection and self-expression, it is important to consider how they might affect our privacy, social interactions, and self-perception. Understanding online self-representation critically and using these tools in an ethical and responsible manner are crucial as technology advances.

7.4 The Idea of "Digital Selves" and How They Connect to Actual Identities

As social media and the internet have grown in popularity, *"digital selves,"* or online personas of people who exist in the virtual world, have emerged. Through our online interactions, content sharing, and self-presentation, these digital selves are actively created and curated rather than merely being passive reflections of our real-world identities. This paper will investigate the idea of *"digital selves,"* looking at their traits, connections to physical identities, and effects on our sense of self.

Qualities of Digital Persons

Several essential characteristics define digital selves:

Curated self-presentation: To project a specific image or message online, people meticulously choose and display data, images, and other content.
Social interaction and validation: People can connect with others, look for validation, and form relationships through online platforms.
Identity experimentation and exploration: People can experiment with various identities, discover new hobbies, and express themselves creatively in the digital sphere.
Persistence and visibility: Internet content has the capacity to endure indefinitely and be widely viewed, thereby forming people's online personas and affecting how other people view them.

Connection to Actual Identities

Real-world identities and digital selves have a complicated and nuanced relationship. Even though our online and offline lives are becoming more and more entwined, our digital selves are not exact replicas of who we are in the real world. Rather, they are frequently edited and romanticized representations of ourselves that show how we would like to be seen by others.

The intricate relationship between digital and real-world identities is influenced by a number of factors:

Selective self-presentation: People decide which facets of their offline identities to highlight online, frequently emphasizing their positive traits while downplaying their negative ones.

Social context: Depending on the platform and target audience, our online personas can change, resulting in distinct digital identities across various online platforms.

Feedback and validation: The comments and affirmations we get online have the power to affect how we see ourselves and how we behave in the real world.

Effects on Our Self-Concept

Our sense of self can be significantly impacted by the process of creating and maintaining digital selves. It can offer chances for exploration, connection, and self-expression, but it can also present difficulties.

Increased self-awareness and self-discovery: Creating and presenting online personas can bring about an increase in self-awareness and self-discovery.
Enhanced community building and social connection: People can feel more a part of a community and connect with others through online platforms.
Possibility of deceit and misrepresentation: Since people may present exaggerated or idealized versions of themselves, the capacity to curate online personas can also result in deceit or misrepresentation.

Effect on offline identity and self-perception: People's offline identities and self-perception may be impacted by their continuous online identity performance, which may cause a gap between their online and offline selves.

In the digital age, our digital selves have become an essential part of our lives, influencing the way we communicate, connect, and express ourselves. Even though they present previously unheard-of chances for identity exploration and self-expression, it is important to consider how they might affect our sense of self and to aim for balance and authenticity in both our online and offline lives. It will be fascinating to observe how the idea of digital selves continues to influence identity and interpersonal relationships as technology develops.

7.5 Identity's Flexibility and Malleability in Online Environments

Investigating the flexibility and malleability of identity has become increasingly popular in the digital sphere. Online spaces give people previously unheard-of chances to experiment with, adapt, and even reinvent themselves, in contrast to the nature of offline identities, which are limited by physical embodiment and social contexts. This essay will look at the different ways that identity becomes flexible and changeable on the internet, analyzing the causes and the effects on one's own self-perception and the wider societal repercussions.

Factors Affecting Online Identity Fluidity:

Online identities are flexible and changeable due to a number of important factors:

Disembodiment: People can separate their online identities from their physical characteristics, such as gender, age, race, or appearance, because they are not physically present in many online interactions. Experimentation with identities that might be restricted in offline contexts is made possible by this deed.

Anonymity and pseudonymity: People can explore various facets of themselves without worrying about social criticism or real-world consequences when they choose to use anonymous or pseudonymous accounts. More candor and openness as well as trying out various personas may result from this.

Curated self-presentation: Online resources give users the ability to selectively choose and highlight certain facets of themselves while leaving out others. This makes it possible to explore various aspects of one's personality or to create idealized or aspirational selves.

Contextual adaptation: People frequently modify their online personas to fit various virtual environments. A person's online persona on a professional networking site is probably going to be different from their online persona on a social media site or in an online gaming community. Because people change their online personas based on the social setting, this contextual adaptation illustrates how fluid online identities are.

Interactivity and feedback: People's perceptions of themselves and their online identities can be shaped by the continuous feedback they receive from others through online interactions. One's online persona may continue to evolve as a result of this feedback loop.

Identity Fluidity Mechanisms:

Online identity fluidity is demonstrated by a number of mechanisms:

Customization and profile creation: Users create digital self-portraits by selecting shared content, bios, and profile pictures that project a specific image.

Creation and modification of avatars: Avatars are visual representations of users in virtual worlds and online games, enabling a great deal of personalization and experimentation with gender, appearance, and other identity markers.

Textual and visual communication: People's online persona is influenced by the way they communicate via text, photos, videos, and other media. Others' perceptions of them are influenced by their language use, tone, and shared content.

Participation in communities: Taking part in various online communities exposes people to a range of viewpoints and social standards, which can have an impact on their own identities and actions.

Consequences for Social Interaction and Self-Perception:

Social interaction and self-perception are significantly impacted by the flexibility and malleability of online identity.

Self-discovery and identity exploration: Internet platforms can offer people a priceless chance to investigate various facets of themselves, which can increase their self-awareness.

Improved community development and social interaction: Online platforms can help people connect with people who have similar values or interests, which promotes a feeling of belonging.

Possibility of deception and misrepresentation: There are worries regarding deception and misrepresentation because it is so simple for people to fabricate or idealize online personas.

Effect on offline identity: People's offline identities and self-perception may be impacted by their continuous performance of online personas, which may cause a gap between their online and offline selves.

Social and psychological effects: Anxiety, stress, or a distorted sense of self are just a few of the social and psychological effects that can result from the pressure to uphold multiple online identities or to follow online social norms.

Online environments have developed into potent testing grounds for identity exploration and experimentation. People have never-before-seen possibilities for self-expression, social interaction, and personal development thanks to the flexibility and malleability of online identities. But it's important to be aware of the possible drawbacks and repercussions of this flexibility, like deceit, misrepresentation, and the effect on offline identity. Fostering a critical understanding of how identity is constructed and performed in the digital age is crucial as technology advances and new online platforms appear.

Chapter 8:

The Ethics of Remixing: Appropriation, Authorship, and Ownership

In today's culture, remixing—the act of taking existing works and turning them into something new—has become a ubiquitous phenomenon. Remixing has challenged conventional ideas of authorship and ownership by obfuscating the distinction between creator and consumer in a variety of media, including literature, film, music, and visual arts. This essay will examine the ideas of appropriation, authorship, and ownership in the context of this dynamic creative practice, delving into the intricate ethical issues surrounding remixing.

Is Appropriation Stealing or Borrowing?

A key component of remixing is appropriation, which is the process of using preexisting sounds, images, or concepts from other sources in original works. But it can be difficult to distinguish between unethical stealing and creative borrowing.

The ethicality of appropriation is determined by a number of factors:

Transformative use: A remix is more likely to be regarded as transformative and, thus, ethical if it gives the original content a new meaning, expression, or purpose.

Attribution and credit: Ethical appropriation requires that the original creator be properly credited. This prevents plagiarism and gives credit to the original author of the content.

Context and intent: The ethicality of a remix is also influenced by the context in which it is presented as well as the remixer's intentions. It is usually regarded as more moral to use a sample for teaching than to use it for profit without authorization.

Writer: Who is the Author?

By questioning who the real creator of a remixed work is, remixing calls into question established ideas of authorship. Who changed the source material—the remixer, the original creator, or both?

There are various viewpoints on this matter:

Original creator: Since the remixed work is based on the original creator's work, some contend that the original creator still maintains primary authorship.
Remixer as author: Some contend that because the remixer has altered the original material and added their own creative touch, they are now the author of the new piece.
Collaborative authorship: According to a third viewpoint, both the original creator and the remixer share authorship, recognizing their respective contributions.

Ownership: Fair Use and Copyright

By granting authors the sole right to their original works, copyright law shields them from unapproved use. However, some uses of copyrighted content, including criticism, commentary, parody, and education, is permitted without permission under the fair use doctrine.

Remixing and copyright law are complicated and hotly contested topics.

A number of considerations must be made in order to decide whether a specific remix qualifies as fair use, including:

The use's intent and nature, including its transformative potential and whether it is commercial or noncommercial.
The type of work protected by copyright: the kind of work—creative or factual—that is being used.
The size and weight of the portion utilized: the extent to which the copyrighted work was utilized.
The impact of the use on the copyrighted work's value or prospective market: if the original work's market is harmed by the use.

Ethical Aspects of Various Remixing Techniques

Depending on the type of remixing, there may be different ethical considerations:

Music sampling: Using brief snippets of pre-existing recordings is a common practice in music sampling, which raises concerns regarding fair use and copyright violations.

Visual arts appropriation: When using pre-existing images or artworks, artists must think about the moral ramifications of their use, make sure they are altering the original work, and give due credit.

Even though fan fiction and fan art are frequently regarded as transformative and noncommercial, they may nevertheless give rise to copyright issues if they make unapproved use of copyrighted characters or plots.

Remixing ethics are intricate and multidimensional, encompassing ownership, authorship, and appropriation considerations. Remixing can be a potent creative outlet, but it's important to consider the moral ramifications and aim for responsible, transformative use of previously created works. We can promote a creative atmosphere that honors the rights of original creators as well as the transformational potential of remixing by having meaningful conversations and creating unambiguous ethical standards.

8.1 What Remix Culture Has to Offer in Terms of Ethics

One of the hallmarks of modern culture is remixing, which is the creative reworking of preexisting works. Remixing has democratized creative expression and questioned conventional ideas of authorship and originality, as seen in everything from music mashups to fan fiction and digital art. But there are some complex ethical issues with this dynamic practice. The ethical issues surrounding remixing will be covered in detail in this essay, along with the subtleties of appropriation, authorship, ownership, and the constantly shifting balance between respect for original works and creative freedom.

Appropriation: An Act of Balance

The act of appropriation, or using preexisting elements in a new creation, is at the core of remixing. Appropriation raises moral concerns about how much it is acceptable to borrow from others, even though it can be a potent tool for creating new meanings and viewpoints. Finding a balance between creative borrowing and outright stealing is crucial.

The morality of appropriation is determined by a number of factors:

Transformative Use: Whether the remixed piece enhances the original is the most important consideration. Plagiarism or copyright violations may result from simply reproducing or slightly altering the borrowed content. However, the remix is more likely to be regarded as ethically sound and fair use if it changes the original content by adding new meaning, expression, or purpose.

Credit and Attribution: Ethical appropriation requires accurate credit. By acknowledging the original creator, the remixer avoids giving the impression that they are the only owner of the material they have borrowed.

Context and Intent: The ethicality of a remix is also influenced by the context in which it is presented as well as the remixer's intentions. Generally speaking, it is more morally acceptable to use a sample for teaching or making a parody than to use it for profit without authorization.

Authorship: A Joint Project

By questioning who the real creator of a remixed work is, remixing calls into question established ideas of authorship. Who changed the source?

material—the remixer, the original creator, or both?

Frequently, the response is intricate and multidimensional. Remixing can be viewed as a cooperative process in which the remixer builds on the foundation laid by the original creator. According to this perspective, both authors contribute to the finished product, and authorship is shared.

Nevertheless, the extent of change also matters. The remixer might be regarded as the main author of the new work if they substantially change the original material while adding a significant amount of new content or meaning. On the other hand, the original creator might still be considered the primary author if the remix only slightly alters the original.

Ownership: Handling Fair Use and Copyright

By granting authors the sole right to their original works, copyright law shields them from unapproved use. However, some uses of copyrighted content, including criticism, commentary, parody, and education, are permitted without permission under the fair use doctrine.

Remixing and copyright law are frequently complicated and contentious issues.

A number of considerations must be made in order to decide whether a specific remix qualifies as fair use, including:

The use's intent and nature, including its transformative potential and whether it is commercial or noncommercial.
The type of work protected by copyright: the kind of work—creative or factual—that is being used.
The size and weight of the portion utilized: the extent to which the copyrighted work was utilized.
The impact of the use on the copyrighted work's value or prospective market: if the original work's market is harmed by the use.

These elements are frequently arbitrary and interpretive, which can result in disagreements over ethics and the law.

Ethical Aspects of Various Remixing Techniques

Depending on the type of remixing, there may be different ethical considerations:

Music Sampling: Using brief snippets of pre-existing recordings is a common practice in music sampling, which raises concerns regarding fair use and copyright violations. Getting consent from the copyright holder or using samples that are obviously transformative are common ethical sampling procedures.

Visual Arts Appropriation: When artists use pre-existing images or artworks, they must think about the moral ramifications of their use, make sure they are altering the original work, and give due credit.

Fan fiction and fan art are frequently regarded as transformative and noncommercial, but they can still give rise to copyright issues if they use storylines or characters that are protected by copyright without authorization. Since their work is noncommercial and transformative, ethical fan creators frequently operate in a gray area.

Remixing ethics are intricate and multidimensional, encompassing ownership, authorship, and appropriation considerations. Remixing can be a potent creative outlet, but it's important to consider the moral ramifications and aim for responsible, transformative use of previously created works. We can promote a creative atmosphere that honors the rights of original creators as well as the transformational potential of remixing by having meaningful conversations and creating unambiguous ethical standards.

8.2 The Argument Between Inspiration and Appropriation

The distinction between inspiration and appropriation can be incredibly blurry in the creative industry. Although they both rely on pre-existing sources, their artistic and ethical implications are very different. Most people view inspiration as a constructive force that fosters creativity and produces original works. Conversely, appropriation frequently evokes negative feelings, implying a lack of creativity and possibly violating intellectual property rights. The intricate argument between appropriation and inspiration will be examined in this essay, along with its main differences, moral implications, and changing viewpoints in the digital era.

Defining Appropriation and Inspiration

The process of being mentally stimulated to do or feel something, particularly to do something creative, is called inspiration. One It entails taking inspiration from different places and combining it to create something fresh and unique. A feeling of enthusiasm, drive, and creative flow are frequently used to describe inspiration.

The act of taking something from a source and repurposing it, frequently without consent or due credit, is known as appropriation. Appropriation in the context of art can refer to the use of preexisting objects, texts, or images in new works of art. In other artistic disciplines, it may entail stealing design elements, modifying narratives, or sampling music.

Important Differences

The following crucial differences aid in distinguishing between appropriation and inspiration:

Transformation: Usually, inspiration results in the development of something truly novel and revolutionary. Even though there may be obvious influences from other works, the finished product is unique and unique. Conversely, appropriation frequently entails little alteration, leaving the original source material largely intact.

Credit and attribution: Since inspiration is frequently diffused and incorporated into the new work, it usually doesn't need to be explicitly attributed. To prevent plagiarism or copyright violations, appropriation necessitates appropriate attribution and consent, particularly when working with copyrighted content.

Context and intent: Two other important factors are the creator's intention and the setting in which the work is displayed. It is more likely to be regarded as inspiration if the goal is to produce something fresh and unique while referencing a variety of sources. It is more likely to be deemed appropriation if the goal is to merely copy or reuse preexisting content without significantly adding value.

Moral Aspects to Take into Account

The moral ramifications of inspiration versus appropriation are nuanced and frequently contested.

A few important ethical factors are as follows:

Unauthorized use of copyrighted content can be considered copyright infringement, which is against the law and unethical.

Plagiarism: In academic and creative contexts, presenting someone else's work as your own is a major ethical transgression.

Cultural appropriation is the term used to describe the taking of aspects of another culture without due respect or understanding, which can be offensive and damaging.

Lack of originality: Reusing preexisting content without significantly enhancing it can be interpreted as a sign of a lack of creativity and originality.

Changing Attitudes in the Digital Era

The argument between inspiration and appropriation has become even more complex in the digital age. The distinction between borrowing and stealing has become more hazy due to the ease with which digital content can be shared, copied, and altered.

The following elements add to this complexity:

The use of pre-existing material in new creative works has become more commonplace due to the rise of sampling and remix culture, which has led to concerns about the limits of transformative and fair use.

Online sharing and dissemination: It is now more challenging to trace the provenance of creative works and to enforce copyright due to the ease with which content can be shared online.

The democratization of creativity: More people are now able to produce and distribute their work thanks to the availability of digital tools, which has increased the variety of influences and interpretations.

The argument between inspiration and appropriation is a significant and continuous topic in the creative community. Although there isn't a simple solution for every problem, creators can better navigate this complicated environment by being aware of the main differences, moral dilemmas, and changing viewpoints in the digital age. Creators can make sure that their use of preexisting material is viewed as inspiration rather than appropriation by aiming for transformation, providing appropriate credit, and being aware of the context and intent of their work.

8.3 The Ownership and Authorship Issue in Remixed Works

Remix culture, in which preexisting works are altered and rearranged to create new ones, has exploded as a result of the development of digital technologies and the internet. Due to the blurring of authorship and ownership boundaries caused by this practice, it is now difficult to determine who is entitled to creative credit and who owns the rights to these remixed works.

Conventional Copyright and Authorship

The person who creates a creative work has historically been regarded as the author. By giving authors the sole authority over their original works—whether they be literary, artistic, musical, or dramatic—copyright law supports this idea. These rights cover the creation of derivative works as well as the reproduction, distribution, performance, and display rights.

Remixing, however, calls into question this conventional authorship paradigm. The boundaries of authorship are blurred when an existing work is altered, looped, or sampled to produce something new. Does the original creator still have some claim to authorship, or is the remixer the new work's author?

The Transformational Role

The level of transformation is a crucial determinant of authorship in remixed works. The original creator is more likely to be regarded as the author if the remixed work merely copies or reproduces the original without significantly altering its expression or meaning. However, the remixer might be regarded as the author of the new work if the original material is significantly changed by the remix, adding new creative elements and changing its meaning or purpose.

Exceptions for Fair Use and Copyright

There are restrictions and exceptions to copyright law, such as fair use, which permits specific uses of content protected by copyright without the owner's consent. The goal of fair use is to strike a balance between the public interest in encouraging creativity and innovation and the rights of creators.

If the remixed work is transformative, noncommercial, and does not negatively impact the original work's market, fair use may be applicable in this situation. However, the four fair use factors must be carefully examined because the application of fair use to remixing is frequently intricate and fact-specific.

Creative Commons and Collaborative Authorship

Recognizing collaborative authorship is an additional strategy for handling authorship in remixed works. This recognizes that the remixer and the original creator should share authorship because they both contributed to the new work.

A versatile framework for copyright management and encouraging collaborative authorship is provided by Creative Commons licenses. With these licenses, authors can give others specific permissions while keeping some of their own rights. A Creative Commons license, for instance, might permit noncommercial uses of a work as long as the original author is credited.

The Value of Credit and Attribution

Attribution and credit are crucial ethical considerations in remixing, regardless of the legal complexities. By properly acknowledging the original creator, plagiarism is prevented and their contribution is acknowledged.

Depending on the context and medium, attribution can take many different forms. In music, it could entail adding the artist and title of the original song to the metadata of the remix. In the visual arts, this could entail mentioning the original piece of art in the exhibition catalog.

Ownership and authorship issues in remixed works are intricate and multidimensional. Every situation must be assessed on its own merits; there is no one-size-fits-all solution. However, we can negotiate this complicated terrain and promote a creative atmosphere that honors both the rights of original creators and the transformative potential of remixing by taking into account the extent of transformation, the application of fair use, the potential for collaborative authorship, and the significance of attribution.

8.4 The Value of Citations and Attribution to Original Sources

Attribution, or giving credit to original sources, is a fundamental ethical practice in the fields of academic research, creative expression, and journalistic integrity. It discourages plagiarism, fosters accountability and transparency, and recognizes the creative and intellectual contributions of others. The multifaceted significance of attribution will be examined in this essay, along with its application in a variety of fields and its role in promoting an intellectual property-respecting culture.

Scholarly discourse and academic integrity

Attribution is essential to preserving integrity and respecting the rules of scholarly discourse in academic research. Researchers are required to properly cite any ideas, information, or findings they use from other sources.

This practice accomplishes multiple goals:

Recognizing intellectual debt: Citations recognize the contributions made by earlier researchers to the field and acknowledge the intellectual debt owed to them.

Avoiding plagiarism: Presenting someone else's work as your own is known as plagiarism, and it can be avoided with proper attribution.

Setting the scene and bolstering assertions: Citations set the scene for the study and bolster the author's assertions.

Enabling verification and additional research: Citations give readers the opportunity to check the accuracy of the information provided and delve deeper into the subject by looking up the original sources.

Inspiration for Art and Creative Expression

Attribution is essential in the creative arts to recognize the sources of inspiration and avoid plagiarism charges. Artists should acknowledge the original authors when they take inspiration from preexisting works, particularly when they use direct quotations, samples, or adaptations. By recognizing its influences, this practice not only shows respect for the original artists but also adds depth and richness to the new work.

Public Trust and Journalistic Ethics

Attribution is crucial to journalism in order to preserve truthfulness, openness, and public confidence. Whether an article is a direct quote, a statistic, or background information, journalists have a duty to credit the original source. By doing this, readers are able to evaluate the reliability of the material and create their own opinions.

Considering the Law and Ethics

In many situations, attribution is required by law in addition to ethical considerations. Original works are protected from unauthorized use by copyright law, and using copyrighted content without authorization or due credit may result in legal repercussions.

A copyright doctrine known as *"fair use"* permits limited, unpermitted uses of copyrighted content for teaching, research, scholarship, news reporting, criticism, and commentary. Nonetheless, correct attribution 1 is still necessary even in situations involving fair use.

The Repercussions of Not Attributing Sources

There may be major ethical and professional repercussions if sources are not cited:

Plagiarism: Passing off someone else's work as your own can result in reputational harm, professional ramifications, and academic sanctions.

Copyright infringement: Unauthorized use of copyrighted content may lead to legal action, including fines and lawsuits.

Credibility loss: In both academic and professional contexts, failing to properly credit sources can harm one's reputation for reliability and credibility.

Top Techniques for Attribution

Proper attribution can be ensured by following a few best practices:

Use citation styles: To guarantee accuracy and consistency in citations, adhere to recognized citation styles like MLA, APA, or Chicago.
For direct quotes, enclose them in quote marks. Provide a reference to the original source and enclose direct quotes in quote marks.
Carefully paraphrase: When you paraphrase, make sure to include a reference to the original source and reword the original text in your own words.
Make use of endnotes or footnotes. To add context or more information to citations, use endnotes or footnotes.
Make use of bibliographies or reference lists: At the conclusion of your work, include a bibliography or reference list that includes all of the sources you have used.

The foundational idea of attribution supports journalistic ethics, artistic expression, and academic integrity. It encourages accountability and transparency, discourages plagiarism, and recognizes the contributions of others. We can promote a culture of respect for intellectual property and guarantee that credit is given where credit is due by adhering to best practices for attribution.

8.5 Getting Around the Ethical Remixing Gray Areas

Remixing has become a common way for people to express themselves creatively in the ever-changing world of digital media. There are now exciting new opportunities for artistic innovation and cultural commentary due to the ability to modify and repurpose existing content. Remixing, however, also brings up difficult moral dilemmas that frequently lie in a *"gray area,"* where definitive solutions are hard to come by. In order to address these ethical ambiguities, this essay will examine the difficulties in managing authorship, copyright, transformative use, and cultural sensitivity within the framework of remix culture.

Fair Use and Copyright: A Juggling Act

By granting authors the sole right to their original works, copyright law shields them from unapproved use. Nonetheless, there are some exceptions under the fair use doctrine which permit restricted, unapproved uses of copyrighted content for things like education, parody, criticism, and commentary.

A complicated four-factor test is used to determine whether a remix is considered fair use:

The intent and nature of the use: Can you tell if the remix is commercial or not? Does it change the original work by giving it a new meaning or purpose?

The type of work protected by copyright: Is the original work imaginative or factual? Has it been released before?

The size and weight of the portion utilized: To what extent did the remix incorporate elements of the original work? Was the used section the ***"heart"*** of the piece?

The impact of the use on the copyrighted work's value or prospective market: Does the original work's or its derivatives' market share suffer as a result of the remix?

No one of these factors is decisive; instead, they are all considered in a balancing test. The ***"gray area"*** of ethical remixing is exacerbated by this innate subjectivity.

Ownership and Authorship: Ignoring the Differences

Conventional ideas of authorship and ownership are called into question by remixing. Who can claim authorship of a work that has undergone significant transformation? Is it the remixer, the original creator, or both?

Likewise, it may not always be clear who owns the remixed piece. Does the remixer acquire ownership of the new work, or does the original copyright holder keep ownership of their original work? When commercial interests are involved, these issues become even more complicated.

Transformative Use: Interpretation Is Key

A fundamental idea in fair use analysis is transformative use. A transformative use is one that gives the original work a new meaning, expression, or objective. However, it's frequently up for interpretation as to whether a given remix is sufficiently transformative to be considered fair use.

While some remixes merely repurpose the original content in a different context, others may obviously offer new commentary or meaning. Because the extent of change can be arbitrary, it can be challenging to distinguish between copyright infringement and fair use.

Cultural Sensitivity: Honoring Various Opinions

Taking cultural sensitivity into account is another aspect of ethical remixing. Being aware of cultural context is crucial when remixing works from other cultures in order to prevent trivialization, appropriation, or misrepresentation.

In order to use the original work in a respectful and significant way, remixers should make an effort to comprehend its cultural significance. This may entail consulting with cultural experts or working with people from the original culture.

Handling the Inconsistencies: A Case-by-Case Method

A case-by-case approach is necessary to navigate the gray areas of ethical remixing because of the intricacies and ambiguities involved. There are no universal rules or simple solutions.

The following elements should be carefully taken into account by creators:

The remix's goal and intention: Does the remix have noncommercial or commercial use in mind? Is the original content to be repurposed or is it to be given a new meaning?
The original work's characteristics: Is the original work imaginative or factual? Is it well-known or comparatively unknown?
The size and weight of the portion utilized: To what extent does the remix incorporate elements of the original work? Is the used section the *"heart"* of the piece?
The possible effect on the original work's market: Does the original work's market value suffer or is it in competition with the remix?
The original work's cultural context: Does the remix honor the original work's cultural significance?

Creators can successfully negotiate the murky waters of ethical remixing and produce works that are both inventive and responsible by carefully weighing these considerations and having meaningful conversations.

Chapter 9:

The Future of Remixing: AI, Algorithms, and Beyond

For many years, the art of remixing—the process of turning preexisting works into new ones—has been a major force behind cultural innovation. New forms of artistic expression and cultural commentary have emerged as a result of remixing, which has blurred the boundaries between creator and consumer in everything from music sampling to film adaptations. The future of remixing is set for even more drastic change as technology continues to develop at an unprecedented rate, with algorithms and artificial intelligence (AI) playing a bigger and bigger role.

Remixing Driven by AI: A New Age of Creative Potential

The ability of AI algorithms to analyze, comprehend, and produce creative content has been astounding.

AI can be applied to remixing in the following ways:

Analyze enormous datasets of previously published works: AI systems are capable of sorting through enormous volumes of data to find themes, patterns, and stylistic components that can be utilized in remixes.

Create new content based on preexisting styles: AI can be trained on particular musicians or genres to produce new material that imitates their aesthetic, resulting in AI-driven parodies or tributes.

Automate complex editing tasks: Artificial intelligence (AI) can automate time-consuming and tiresome editing tasks, like splicing, cutting, and modifying audio or video, allowing human creators to concentrate on more imaginative remixing techniques.

Make customized remixes: AI can produce remixes based on user preferences, giving customers one-of-a-kind, customized experiences.

Algorithmic Curation and Discovery: Broadening Mix Culture's Audience

In addition to AI's creative potential, algorithms are becoming more and more significant in the distribution and curation of remixed content. Algorithms are used by recommendation systems on social media feeds, streaming platforms, and search engines to present users with interesting and relevant content, thereby extending the reach of remix culture and introducing creators to new audiences.

Legal and Ethical Issues: Getting Started in Unknown Fields

There are several ethical and legal issues that need to be addressed in light of the growing popularity of AI-powered remixing. Because it was created for a world with human creators, copyright law finds it difficult to keep up with the quick developments in artificial intelligence. When AI is incorporated into the creative process, issues of authorship, ownership, and fair use become even more complicated.

Concerns regarding representation, bias, and the possibility of abuse of AI-generated content must also be carefully taken into account. Establishing moral standards and legislative frameworks that guarantee the responsible and fair use of AI in the context of remixing is essential as the technology advances.

The Changing Function of Human Artists: Cooperation and Curation

Even though AI and algorithms are expected to have a big impact on remixing in the future, human creators will always be crucial. Choosing source material, directing the creative process of remixes, and giving them emotional resonance and meaning still heavily relies on human creativity, intuition, and cultural awareness.

It's possible that human-AI cooperation will increase in the future, with AI tools enhancing rather than completely replacing human creativity. In order to produce coherent and captivating remixes, human creators may also adopt a more curatorial role, choosing and honing AI-generated material.

Democratizing Creativity: Giving Voices to New Generations

The availability of algorithmic platforms and AI tools could further democratize creativity by enabling people from diverse backgrounds to engage in remix culture. The barriers to entry for creative expression will continue to decline as AI helps with intricate editing tasks and algorithms link creators and audiences.

A more inclusive and varied cultural environment where fresh viewpoints and voices are valued and amplified may result from this democratization of creativity.

Leveraging Remixing's Transformative Potential

AI and algorithms have the potential to open up new creative avenues and broaden the appeal of remix culture, so the future of remixing looks bright. We can ensure that remixing remains a potent tool for creativity, cultural criticism, and artistic expression in the future by embracing these technological developments while tackling the moral and legal issues they raise.

9.1 Examining the Possible Effects of Algorithms and Artificial Intelligence on Remixing

Technological developments have had a big impact on remixing, the creative process of repurposing existing works. The field of remixing is currently on the verge of another significant change due to the quick advancement of artificial intelligence (AI) and complex algorithms. The possible effects of AI and algorithms on remixing in a variety of artistic fields will be discussed in this essay, along with the associated opportunities, difficulties, and wider ramifications for society, culture, and the arts.

AI's Ingenious Remixing Potential

The remixing process could be completely transformed by AI algorithms' potent capabilities:

Automated Content Analysis: AI is able to examine enormous text, image, audio, and video datasets to find themes, patterns, and stylistic components that human creators might miss. By revealing hidden connections between seemingly unrelated works, this automated analysis can generate fresh remix ideas.

Generative Adversarial Networks (GANs) and transformers are examples of generative AI models that can produce new content by using patterns they have learned. This could involve writing new chapters that expand on existing novels, creating new scenes based on existing film footage, or coming up with variations of existing melodies.

Intelligent Content Manipulation: AI is capable of automating intricate editing processes like image manipulation, video editing, and audio mixing. Human creators can now concentrate on more complex creative choices like story design and conceptualization.

Customized Remix Experiences: AI is able to customize remixes to suit personal tastes. Consider an AI that creates customized playlists that skillfully combine various artists and genres by remixing music based on your listening history.

Algorithms and Remixed Content Distribution

Algorithms are essential for the dissemination and discovery of remixed works in addition to content creation:

Recommendation Systems: Using algorithms, websites such as YouTube, Spotify, and TikTok suggest content to users based on their listening or viewing preferences. Users may be introduced to a greater variety of remixed works as a result, which they might not otherwise find. Algorithms are also employed for content filtering and moderation, which can affect remix culture in both positive and negative ways. Although algorithms can aid in stopping the dissemination of damaging or illegal content, they may also unintentionally restrict legal remixes or inhibit artistic expression.

Algorithmic Curation: By assembling collections of remixed works according to particular themes, styles, or trends, algorithms can open up new avenues for exploration.

Difficulties and Moral Aspects

A number of difficulties and moral dilemmas are also raised by the incorporation of AI and algorithms into remixing:

Copyright and Ownership: AI-generated content is outpacing the copyright legal framework. Who is the owner of the copyright to an AI-generated remix—the AI developer, the original creator, or the person who triggered the AI?

Authorship and Creative Control: Authorship and creative control issues become more complicated as AI becomes more involved in the creative process. What level of human involvement is necessary for a remix to qualify as a human creation?

Representation and Bias: Since AI algorithms are trained on preexisting data, they may exhibit preexisting biases and disparities. This may result in the exclusion of particular voices or viewpoints from remixed works or the continuation of damaging stereotypes.

The Loss of Human Touch: Some argue that AI-generated remixes lack the human touch, the emotional depth, and the cultural understanding that are essential to truly meaningful creative expression.

The Changing Function of Human Innovators

Even with AI's growing powers, human creators will continue to play a vital role in remixing.

Human ingenuity, instinct, and cultural awareness are still crucial for:

Conceptualization and Vision: In order to choose suitable source material, decide on the intended result, and establish the general concept and vision for a remix, human creators are required.
Curatorial Decisions: AI-generated content can be chosen and improved by human creators to produce coherent and captivating remixes.
Emotional and Cultural Contextualization: Remixes can be given layers of meaning that AI alone cannot duplicate by human creators who can infuse them with emotional nuance and cultural awareness.

Remixing's Future: A Hybrid Strategy

The most likely future of remixing is a hybrid one in which human creators collaborate with

AI and algorithms. The repetitive and technical tasks can be handled by AI, allowing human creators to concentrate on the more imaginative and creative elements of remixing. This partnership has the potential to open up previously unthinkable avenues for creative expression.

The creative landscape could be completely changed by the incorporation of AI and algorithms into remixing, which would present fascinating new chances for artistic innovation and cross-cultural interaction. Addressing the moral and legal issues raised by this technological development is essential, though. We can guarantee that the future of remixing is one that encourages creativity, respects intellectual property, and advances a more inclusive and diverse cultural landscape by carefully examining the role of human creators and establishing ethical guidelines.

9.2 The Development of Generative AI and How It Affects Creative Production

The rapid development of generative AI is causing a seismic shift in the creative production landscape. These potent algorithms are upending conventional ideas of authorship, creativity, and the very essence of art itself because they can produce original text, images, music, code, and even videos. The emergence of generative AI will be discussed in this essay, along with its potential applications, ramifications for other creative industries, and wider ethical and societal issues it brings up.

Generative AI's Potential

In a variety of creative fields, generative AI models—especially those built on deep learning architectures such as transformers, variational autoencoders (VAEs), and generative adversarial networks (GANs)—have shown remarkable capabilities.

Text Generation: AI is capable of producing text of human caliber, including scripts, articles, stories, poetry, and even code. These models can generate outputs that are coherent and pertinent to the context by learning the subtleties of language, style, and structure from large text datasets.

Image Generation: AI is capable of producing both realistic and imaginative images, from abstract art and fantastical creatures to photorealistic landscapes and portraits. These models are able to create images that mimic or blend various styles and genres by learning their visual traits.

AI is capable of creating original music in a variety of genres, including melodies, harmonies, and rhythmic patterns. These models are able to produce music that is both unique and stylistically consistent because they can learn the patterns and structures of various genres.

Video Generation: Although AI is still in its infancy, models that can produce short films, animate characters, and even produce lifelike facial expressions are starting to make inroads into this field.

3D Model Generation: The ability of AI to create 3D models of things, people, and settings has important ramifications for the creation of video games, animation, and virtual reality.

Consequences for Creative Industries

Many creative fields will be significantly impacted by the development of generative AI.

AI can be used as a tool for artistic exploration in the fields of art and design, enabling artists to experiment with various styles, come up with new ideas, and produce works that would be impossible to accomplish by hand.

Writing and Journalism: AI can help journalists and writers with tasks like creating individualized content, summarizing information, and producing drafts.

AI has the ability to compose music, produce sound effects, and produce customized soundtracks for movies, video games, and other media.

AI-powered non-player characters (NPCs), dynamic game environments, and game assets can all be produced using AI in video game development.

AI can help with a variety of film and television production tasks, including storyboarding, scriptwriting, visual effects, and even making trailers or short films.

Social and Moral Aspects to Take into Account

The rise of generative AI also raises several important societal and ethical considerations:

Authorship and Ownership: Who has the right to claim authorship and ownership of creative content produced by AI? This brings up difficult philosophical and legal issues regarding intellectual property rights.

Human Creativity's Value: A homogenization of artistic expression and a devaluation of human creativity are two concerns raised by the growing usage of AI-generated content.

AI's potential to automate creative tasks raises concerns about job displacement in the creative industries.

Deepfakes and Misinformation: The potential for abuse, including the production of deepfakes or misinformation, is a concern raised by AI's capacity to produce lifelike images and videos.

Representation and Bias: Since AI models are trained on preexisting data, they may exhibit preexisting biases and disparities. This can lead to the perpetuation of harmful stereotypes or the exclusion of certain voices or perspectives in AI-generated content.

The Future of Creative Production

The future of creative production is likely to involve a collaborative relationship between humans and AI. AI can serve as a powerful tool for augmenting human creativity, assisting with tedious tasks, generating new ideas, and expanding creative possibilities. Nonetheless, human ingenuity, instinct, and cultural awareness will continue to be crucial in determining the course of artistic endeavors and giving them significance and emotional resonance.

The rise of generative AI is transforming the landscape of creative production, offering exciting new opportunities for artistic innovation and cultural expression. Addressing the moral and societal issues raised by this technology is essential, though. We can harness the creative potential of AI while reducing its potential risks by encouraging a careful and responsible approach to its development and application.

9.3 Copyright and Intellectual Property's Future in an AI-Generated Content World

Existing copyright and intellectual property (IP) frameworks are in a state of chaos due to the rapid development of artificial intelligence (AI), especially in the area of generative models that can produce text, images, music, and other types of creative content. The complexity of AI-generated works is difficult for these frameworks to handle because they were primarily created for human authorship. In a world where AI-generated content is becoming more and more prevalent, this essay will examine the difficulties and possible future paths of copyright and intellectual property law.

The Present Situation of AI and Copyright

In general, *"original works of authorship"* that are fixed in a tangible medium of expression are protected by current copyright law. Human authorship is typically implied by this definition. Then, the question arises: is it possible to classify an AI as an *"author"*?

Human Authorship as the Default: Current copyright laws in the majority of jurisdictions mandate human authorship. In general, works produced entirely by AI with little to no human involvement are not protected by copyright.

Human Input as a Basis for Protection: The resultant work may be eligible for copyright protection if a human contributes a substantial amount of creative input to the AI's output, such as choosing training data, offering instructions, or editing and improving the produced content. The scope of this protection and the identity of the rights holders are still complicated matters, though.

Ownership of Training Data: The ownership of the data used to train AI models is another important consideration. Even if the AI-generated output differs greatly from the original works, copyright infringement claims may arise if copyrighted material is used in the training process without authorization.

Problems with Current Frameworks

Existing copyright and intellectual property frameworks face several significant challenges as generative AI grows in popularity:

The identification of the *"author"* becomes more challenging when artificial intelligence (AI) is used in the creative process. Who is the author—the AI itself, the user who gave the prompt, or the AI developer?

Defining Originality: AI-generated content challenges the idea of originality, which is a fundamental component of copyright protection. Can an AI's output be regarded as truly original if it has been trained on a large dataset of previously published works?

Detection and Enforcement: As AI models advance and are able to produce increasingly realistic and unique-looking works, it becomes more difficult to identify AI-generated content and enforce copyright.

Global Harmonization: Different nations have different copyright laws, which further complicates the global digital environment. It will be very difficult to harmonize these laws to deal with AI-generated content.

Possible Paths for IP and Copyright in the Future

To overcome the difficulties presented by AI-generated content, a number of possible strategies are being examined:

Sui Generis Protection: According to some legal experts, a sui generis right is a novel type of intellectual property protection intended exclusively for works produced by artificial intelligence. This could entail different protection criteria, like emphasizing the investment made in creating the AI model instead of conventional ideas of authorship.

Human-in-the-Loop Frameworks: This strategy may work by focusing on human input as the foundation for copyright protection. This would necessitate establishing rules for identifying authorship and ownership in collaborative human-AI creations as well as precisely defining what *"significant human input"* is.

Licensing and Collective Management: The rights of AI-generated content could be managed by adapting current licensing procedures and collective management organizations (CMOs). This can entail developing fresh licensing schemes that take into account the special qualities of works produced by artificial intelligence.

Disclosure and Transparency: Enforcing disclosure of the use of AI in content production may encourage transparency and empower users to choose the media they want to consume with knowledge. This could entail identifying the content as ***"AI-generated"*** or supplying details about the AI model that was employed.

International Cooperation's Significance

International collaboration and harmonization of copyright and intellectual property laws are necessary to address the global ramifications of AI-generated content. For creators, users, and companies functioning in the digital sphere, this will be essential to guaranteeing a uniform and predictable legal framework.

Existing copyright and intellectual property frameworks are facing serious challenges as generative AI gains traction. The complexity of AI-generated content is too great for the conventional emphasis on human authorship and originality. Addressing authorship, ownership, and enforcement concerns will require either modifying current legislation or developing new legal frameworks. Navigating this quickly changing environment and guaranteeing a just and balanced system that encourages innovation and the preservation of creative works will require international cooperation and an emphasis on transparency.

9.4 The Changing Interaction of Machines and Humans in Creative Processes

In creative processes, the interaction between humans and machines has changed dramatically, progressing from basic execution tools to complex collaborators and even autonomous producers of creative content. Significant queries concerning the nature of creativity, the function of human agency, and the prospects for artistic expression are brought up by this changing dynamic. This paper will investigate this dynamic relationship by looking at the historical background, the state of human-machine cooperation today, and the possible future directions of this intricate interaction.

A Historical View of the Transition from Tools to Partners

In the past, machines have enhanced human creativity by augmenting our mental and physical capacities. Machines have made it possible for us to reproduce, distribute, and work with creative works on a scale that was previously unthinkable, from the printing press to the advancement of photography and film.

Initially, machines were essentially tools of execution that performed tasks in accordance with human directives. The musician played the instrument, the writer typed on the typewriter, and the artist used the brush. The machine was a passive tool that enhanced human talent without producing original work of its own.

But the relationship between humans and machines started to change with the introduction of computers and digital technologies. In addition to carrying out commands, computers can now process data, produce patterns, and even produce original content.

The Present Situation: Cooperation Between Humans and Machines

A new era of human-machine cooperation in creative processes is currently underway. Artificial intelligence (AI) algorithms, especially those built on deep learning, have proven to be remarkably adept at producing text, images, music, and other creative content.

This cooperation can take many different forms:

AI as an inspiration and ideation tool: AI can be used to overcome creative blocks, generate new ideas, and explore various creative directions. Artificial intelligence (AI) can, for instance, produce song variations, design color schemes, or story outline ideas.

AI as a partner in the creative process: AI can assist human creators with tasks like mixing, mastering, and editing. AI can be used, for instance, to create realistic special effects for videos, improve audio recordings, and automatically colorize black and white images.

AI as a self-sufficient creator: There are instances when AI can produce imaginative material with little assistance from humans, which raises concerns regarding originality and authorship. For instance, AI is capable of writing poetry, stories, abstract art, and original music in a variety of genres.

The Prospects for Cooperation Between Humans and Machines

Even more integration and interdependence are probably in store for the future of human-machine cooperation in creative processes.

We can expect:

More advanced AI tools: AI models will grow even more potent and adaptable, producing ever-more intricate and subtle creative output.

Smooth integration into creative workflows: AI tools will be easily incorporated into current creative software and workflows, facilitating collaboration between AI and human creators.

Novel forms of artistic expression: The cooperation of AI and humans will give rise to hitherto unthinkable new forms of artistic expression.

A change in the role of human creators: Instead of focusing on producing original content, human creators may now largely curate, oversee, and improve AI-generated content.

Philosophical and Ethical Aspects

A number of significant ethical and philosophical issues are brought up by the changing dynamic between humans and machines in creative processes:

The nature of creativity: Can machines actually be creative? What exactly is creativity? Is content produced by AI merely an advanced form of imitation, or does it represent true creativity?

The importance of human creativity: Will human artistry be diminished and creative expression become more uniform as AI-generated content becomes more widely used?

Ownership and authorship: Who is able to assert ownership and authorship over content produced by artificial intelligence? What changes should be made to copyright law to reflect this new reality?

The effect on the identity of humans: How will our perception of human identity and our interaction with technology change as artificial intelligence becomes more and more integrated into creative processes?

With significant ramifications for the future of art, culture, and society, the dynamic and complex relationship between humans and machines in creative processes is constantly changing. Even though artificial intelligence (AI) has both advantages and disadvantages, it is imperative to approach this technological development with consideration and responsibility. We can preserve the special value of human artistry while opening up new creative possibilities by encouraging human-machine collaboration.

9.5 Hypotheses Regarding Upcoming Developments in Remix Culture

One of the hallmarks of the digital age is remix culture, which is defined by the imaginative repurposing and alteration of pre-existing cultural artifacts. Remixing has influenced a wide range of fields, including literature, visual arts, music, and even scientific research, thanks to changes in social norms and technological advancements. Looking ahead, a number of significant trends are probably going to influence how remix culture develops, pushing its limits and redefining its social impact.

AI-Powered Remixing and Hyperpersonalization:

Remixing is already heavily influenced by artificial intelligence (AI), and this trend is only expected to increase. Hyper-personalization will probably be possible with future AI tools, allowing remixes to be made to suit specific tastes and preferences. Imagine artificial intelligence (AI) algorithms that create original remixes of songs, movies, or even memories based on your viewing preferences, listening history, and even emotional reactions. This degree of customization may give rise to completely new kinds of immersive and interactive experiences.

The Metaverse and Decentralized Remixing's Ascent:

Decentralized platforms and blockchain technology have the potential to completely transform the production, distribution, and commercialization of remixes. Collaborative remixing projects, in which several creators contribute and share ownership of the finished product, may be made possible by decentralized autonomous organizations (DAOs). Users will be able to create and share virtual environments, avatars, and experiences that combine elements from multiple sources thanks to the metaverse's immersive virtual worlds.

Distinguishing Between Digital and Physical Remixing:

The distinction between digital and physical remixing will become more hazy as digital technologies become more integrated into the real world. Users will be able to superimpose digital content onto real-world locations using augmented reality (AR) and virtual reality (VR), resulting in mixed-reality remixes that combine the virtual and the real. Consider using virtual reality (VR) to experience a remixed version of a historical event or augmented reality (AR) to remix your physical surroundings with virtual graffiti.

Remixing as a Political and Social Activism Tool:

For social and political commentary, remixing has always been a potent tool, and this trend is probably here to stay. Using data visualization, deepfakes, and other strategies to reveal injustice, subvert power structures, and encourage social change, future remixes might make use of AI and other technologies to produce more powerful and convincing messages.

The Development of Intellectual Property and Copyright:

Remix culture poses serious problems for the current copyright framework, which was primarily created for a pre-digital era. The collaborative and transformative nature of remixing may require future legal frameworks to change; this could be done by implementing new types of intellectual property protection, extending fair use clauses, or granting Creative Commons licenses.

Remixing as a Way to Reinterpret and Preserve Culture:

In order to preserve and reinterpret cultural heritage, remixing can be extremely important. Creators can guarantee the ongoing relevance of historical artifacts, traditional art forms, and cultural narratives by repurposing them for modern audiences. By evaluating and cataloguing enormous volumes of cultural data, AI could help with this process and give remixers fresh ideas and inspiration.

The Development of Fan Communities and Participatory Remixing:

Fan communities that participate in participatory remixing through fan fiction, fan art, and other fan-generated content have already flourished thanks to the internet. Future platforms and tools will probably allow for even higher levels of participation and collaboration, so this trend is likely to continue.

The democratization of access and creative tools:

Remix culture will become even more accessible with the growing availability of potent creative tools, such as online platforms and AI-powered software. This will enable people from all walks of life to engage in artistic expression and support the continuous repurposing of culture.

Ethical Issues and Conscientious Remixing:

Ethics issues will become even more crucial as remixing gains strength and popularity. It will be necessary to use education, moral principles, and legal frameworks to address issues like copyright infringement, cultural appropriation, and the dissemination of false information.

In the Digital Age, Remixing as a Fundamental Literacy:

In the digital age, the capacity to comprehend, evaluate, and produce remixes might eventually become fundamental literacy. Navigating the complicated digital landscape will require the ability to critically assess and synthesize information and media, which are becoming more and more fragmented and remixed.

Remix culture has a lot of exciting things ahead of it. Remixing will keep changing how we produce, consume, and engage with culture, propelled by advances in technology and shifting social mores. We can make sure that remixing remains a potent force for innovation, cultural commentary, and social change by embracing its creative potential while addressing the moral and legal issues it raises.

Conclusion:

Everything is a Remix? A nuanced Perspective

Because sampling, appropriation, and reinterpretation are so common in modern culture, the phrase *"Everything is a Remix"* has gained popularity in the digital age. Although there is some truth to this statement, it is crucial to approach it nuancedly and refrain from oversimplifying it. The idea of *"Everything is a Remix"* will be examined from a variety of angles in this essay, including its applicability, drawbacks, and consequences for originality and creativity.

Is "Everything is a Remix" Valid?

The notion that everything is a remix stems from the finding that original works of art are rarely created in a vacuum. Whether intentionally or inadvertently, artists, writers, musicians, and other creators incorporate elements from earlier works into their own creations, drawing inspiration from preexisting sources.

This can appear in a number of ways:

Musicians frequently use recordings of previously recorded music to create new songs by fusing vocals, rhythms, or melodies.
Literary and cinematic adaptations: Existing narratives, characters, or themes are reinterpreted by authors and filmmakers for new audiences or settings.
In the visual arts, appropriation occurs when artists take preexisting objects, images, or styles and reinterpret them to produce new works of art.
These illustrations show how creative works frequently build upon earlier ones, resulting in a cascade of reinterpretation and influence. One could argue that everything is a remix in this way.

"Everything is a Remix" has limitations.

Although the idea that *"everything is a remix"* has some merit, it's critical to understand its limitations. Not every creative work is just a remix of something that already exists. Some pieces push the limits of their respective fields with a high level of originality and innovation.

Additionally, the idea that *"Everything is a Remix"* can be abused to excuse copyright violations or plagiarism. Remixing is not the same as simply copying or reproducing existing content without significantly adding new value; this is just theft.

Variations and Differences

It's critical to take into account a number of differences in order to develop a more complex understanding of the connection between remixing and originality:

Degree of transformation: The extent to which remixes alter the original content varies. While some remixes only make small changes or additions; others drastically change the original content to produce something completely different.

Context and intent: Both the creator's intention and the setting in which the work is displayed are significant factors. Remixing is not the same as merely copying or reproducing already-existing content. Nonetheless, it may be regarded as remixing if the goal is to produce something fresh and unique while incorporating different inspirations.

Attribution and credit: Ethical remixing requires giving due credit to the original sources. This refrains from plagiarism while acknowledging the impact of earlier works.

Effects on Originality and Creativity

The idea that *"everything is a remix"* affects our perception of originality and creativity. It suggests that creativity is not about creating something entirely new from scratch but rather about reconfiguring and reinterpreting existing elements in new and innovative ways.

For creators, this viewpoint can be empowering because it implies that they don't have to feel under pressure to produce entirely original work. Alternatively, they can take ideas from pre-existing sources and concentrate on changing and reinterpreting them in their own special way.

By emphasizing the importance of influence and reinterpretation in the production of new works, the statement "Everything is a Remix" encapsulates a significant component of creative practice. But it's crucial to approach this idea nuancedly and refrain from oversimplifying it. It's crucial to distinguish between plagiarism and ethical remixing because not all creative works are just remixes. We can better appreciate the intricate relationship between remixing and originality if we are aware of the subtleties and differences at play.

➤ Reexamining the Main Question: Is Everything a Remix?

The notion that *"Everything is a Remix,"* which was made popular by Kirby Ferguson's documentary series, has become widely accepted in conversations about originality, creativity, and intellectual property in the digital age. It asserts that true originality is a myth and that all creative works are based on pre-existing concepts, forms, and styles. Although this idea is very important, it is important to reexamine this main query from a more nuanced perspective, recognizing both its applicability and its limitations as well as its potential for misunderstanding.

The Main Point: Components of Remixing in Creative Works

"Everything is a Remix" is based on the observation that creativity rarely arises from a void. Inevitably, artists are influenced by their environment, taking in elements from historical

settings, cultural fads, and previously completed works. The core of remixing is the process of taking, altering, and fusing preexisting elements.

Ferguson's documentary emphasizes a number of crucial elements of this procedure, including:

Copying is the act of intentionally or unintentionally reproducing preexisting elements. It can be anything from a straight quote or sample to more subtly influenced form or style.

Transforming entails adding new context, meaning, or expression while changing or modifying already-existing elements. This transformative quality is what sets remixing apart from simple plagiarism or copying.

Combining is the process of fusing components from multiple sources to produce something new. This can result in creative expression that is hybrid, combining media, styles, or genres.

These procedures are evident in a variety of creative fields:

Music: The continuous cycle of remixing is demonstrated by the widespread use of sampling, interpolation, and cover versions.

Television and movies: Remixing in visual media is evident in adaptations, remakes, and sequels, which expand on preexisting plots, characters, and universes.

Literature: Pastiche, intertextuality, and the retelling of myths, legends, and historical events all show how earlier works have influenced new works of literature.

Visual arts: Collage, photomontage, and appropriation art all directly interact with preexisting objects and images, rearranging them to convey new meanings.

Details and Rebuttals: Innovativeness and Originality

Though it offers a useful framework for comprehending creative influence, the

"Everything is a Remix" idea must not be oversimplified. The idea should not be used to excuse plagiarism or a lack of originality because not all creative works are merely remixes.

Numerous subtleties and rebuttals need to be taken into account:

Degree of transformation: It's important to consider how much a work alters its original material. Since it lacks the transformative component that lends remixing its creative value, a simple copy or reproduction is not a remix. A genuine remix introduces something fresh, be it a different viewpoint, a different setting, or a different way of expressing oneself.

What is meant by originality? Certain works exhibit a greater level of innovation and novelty than others, even though complete originality may not exist. These pieces could present novel ideas, methods, or aesthetics that have a big influence on their fields.

The function of human willpower: Although they draw inspiration from previously created works, artists also contribute their own distinct viewpoints, experiences, and creative vision. This human agency plays a crucial role in influencing the remixing process and giving the resulting works significance and emotional resonance.

The Range of Remixing:

Remixing is not so much a binary as a spectrum. Simple reproduction or copying, which has no transformative value and is frequently regarded as plagiarism, is at one extreme of the spectrum. Remixes that drastically change the original material to produce something truly unique and novel are at the other extreme. The majority of creative works fall somewhere in the middle, incorporating both their own original contributions and inspiration from pre-existing sources.

Remix culture is accelerating in the digital age.

The speed and scope of remixing have been greatly increased by the digital age. Remixed works across a variety of media have proliferated due to the ease with which digital content can be copied, shared, and altered. Remixing is a common practice in many online communities, including fan fiction communities, remix music platforms, and meme culture, which have grown in popularity thanks to the internet.

A reasonable viewpoint

A good place to start when trying to understand the dynamics of influence and creativity is with the question, ***"Is Everything a Remix?"*** The idea emphasizes how unquestionably preexisting works influence new works, but it's also critical to acknowledge the significance of change, uniqueness, and human agency. We can better understand the intricate and constantly changing nature of creativity in the digital age by taking a nuanced approach that recognizes both the concept's advantages and disadvantages.

> Is Everything a Remix? Asks the Remix Generation.

"The Remix Generation: Is Everything a Remix?" by Eric Buffett examines how ubiquitous remixing is in modern culture and makes the case that all creative works are based on preexisting concepts, forms, and styles. The history of remixing, its different forms, and its effects on originality, creativity, and intellectual property are all covered in the book.

Important Points

Buffett contends that genuine originality is a myth and that creativity is not original. Every creative endeavor is impacted by earlier creations, and artists invariably find inspiration in their environment. The core of remixing is this process of taking, altering, and fusing preexisting elements.

Remixing is a spectrum: Remixing is a spectrum rather than a binary concept. Simple reproduction or copying is at one extreme, and remixes that drastically change the original content are at the other.

Because digital content is so easily copied, shared, and altered, the number of remixed works has skyrocketed, contributing to the acceleration of remix culture. Remixing is a common practice in online communities that have grown as a result of the internet.

Traditional ideas of authorship and ownership are challenged by remixing. Traditional notions of who is entitled to creative credit and who owns the rights to remixed works are called into question by the collaborative and transformative nature of remixing.

When remixing, ethical considerations are crucial: Remixing can be a potent creative outlet, but it's important to think about the moral ramifications, including copyright violations and cultural appropriation.

Important Results

Remixing has a long history. Remixing is not a new phenomenon. It has been around for centuries in a variety of forms, including literary adaptations and musical variations.

Remixing is a broad practice that includes a variety of artistic endeavors, such as mashups, sampling, adaptation, appropriation, and parody.

Many factors influence remixing: artists remix for a variety of reasons, such as commercial considerations, audience engagement, cultural commentary, and artistic expression.

The media landscape has been profoundly impacted by remixing, which has generated new business models in the entertainment sector, questioned conventional ideas of authorship, and blurred the boundaries between creator and consumer.

The ethical and legal issues surrounding remixing are complicated and multidimensional, and there are no simple solutions. Every case needs to be assessed separately, taking into account the particular circumstances and level of change that are involved.

A useful framework for comprehending the dynamics of influence and creativity in the digital age is offered by ***"The Remix Generation: Is Everything a Remix?"*** It emphasizes the significance of change, uniqueness, and ethical considerations while highlighting the indisputable influence of earlier works on the development of new works. We can better understand the intricate and dynamic nature of creativity in a world increasingly influenced by remix culture by taking the nuanced stance that recognizes the merits and limitations of the *"Everything is a remix"* idea.

➤ Acknowledging the complexities and nuances of remix culture.

One of the hallmarks of the digital age is remix culture, which is defined by the imaginative repurposing and alteration of pre-existing cultural artifacts. Remixing has influenced a wide range of fields, including literature, visual arts, music, and even scientific research, thanks to changes in social norms and technological advancements. Looking ahead, a number of significant trends are probably going to influence how remix culture develops, pushing its limits and redefining its social impact.

AI-Powered Remixing and Hyperpersonalization:

Remixing is already heavily influenced by artificial intelligence (AI), and this trend is only expected to increase. Hyper-personalization will probably be possible with future AI tools, allowing remixes to be made to suit specific tastes and preferences. Imagine artificial intelligence (AI) algorithms that create original remixes of songs, movies, or even memories based on your viewing preferences, listening history, and even emotional reactions. This degree of customization may give rise to completely new kinds of immersive and interactive experiences.

The Metaverse and Decentralized Remixing's Ascent:

Decentralized platforms and blockchain technology have the potential to completely transform the production, distribution, and commercialization of remixes. Collaborative remixing projects, in which several creators contribute and share ownership of the finished product, may be made possible by decentralized autonomous organizations (DAOs). Users will be able to create and share virtual environments, avatars, and experiences that combine elements from multiple sources thanks to the metaverse's immersive virtual worlds.

Distinguishing Between Digital and Physical Remixing:

The distinction between digital and physical remixing will become more hazy as digital technologies become more integrated into the real world. Users will be able to superimpose digital content onto real-world locations using augmented reality (AR) and virtual reality (VR), resulting in mixed-reality remixes that combine the virtual and the real. Consider using virtual reality (VR) to experience a remixed version of a historical event or augmented reality (AR) to remix your physical surroundings with virtual graffiti.

Remixing as a Political and Social Activism Tool:

For social and political commentary, remixing has always been a potent tool, and this trend is probably here to stay. Using data visualization, deepfakes, and other strategies to reveal injustice, subvert power structures, and encourage social change, future remixes might make use of AI and other technologies to produce more powerful and convincing messages.

The Development of Intellectual Property and Copyright:

Remix culture poses serious problems for the current copyright framework, which was primarily created for a pre-digital era. The collaborative and transformative nature of remixing may require future legal frameworks to change; this could be done by implementing new types of intellectual property protection, extending fair use clauses, or granting Creative Commons licenses.

Remixing as a Way to Reinterpret and Preserve Culture:

In order to preserve and reinterpret cultural heritage, remixing can be extremely important. Creators can guarantee the ongoing relevance of historical artifacts, traditional art forms, and cultural narratives by repurposing them for modern audiences. By evaluating and cataloguing enormous volumes of cultural data, AI could help with this process and give remixers fresh ideas and inspiration.

The Development of Fan Communities and Participatory Remixing:

Fan communities that participate in participatory remixing through fan fiction, fan art, and other fan-generated content have already flourished thanks to the internet. Future platforms and tools will probably allow for even higher levels of participation and collaboration, so this trend is likely to continue.

The democratization of access and creative tools:

Remix culture will become even more accessible with the growing availability of potent creative tools, such as online platforms and AI-powered software. This will enable people from all walks of life to engage in artistic expression and support the continuous repurposing of culture.

Ethical Issues and Conscientious Remixing:

Ethics issues will become even more crucial as remixing gains strength and popularity. It will be necessary to use education, moral principles, and legal frameworks to address issues like copyright infringement, cultural appropriation, and the dissemination of false information.

In the Digital Age, Remixing as a Fundamental Literacy:

In the digital age, the capacity to comprehend, evaluate, and produce remixes might eventually become fundamental literacy. Navigating the complicated digital landscape will require the ability to critically assess and synthesize information and media, which are becoming more and more fragmented and remixed.

Remix culture has a lot of exciting things ahead of it. Remixing will keep changing how we produce, consume, and engage with culture, propelled by advances in technology and shifting social mores. We can make sure that remixing remains a potent force for innovation, cultural commentary, and social change by embracing its creative potential while addressing the moral and legal issues it raises.

➤ Providing a Concluding View on the Character of Creativity and Originality in the Digital Age

The digital era has drastically changed how we think about creativity and originality. Traditional ideas of authorship and artistic creation have been called into question by the proliferation of digital tools, the ease of access to information, and the emergence of remix culture. This essay presents a concluding viewpoint on the nature of creativity and originality in this digital age, highlighting the special opportunities and difficulties of the present while also acknowledging the influences of the past.

The Pristine Originality Myth

Bibliography

Eric Buffett's book *"The Remix Generation: Is Everything a Remix?"* explores the intriguing realm of remix culture and its significant influence on originality, creativity, and intellectual property in the digital era. Using a thorough bibliography of sources that support Buffett's analysis, we will examine the main points and conclusions made in the book in this essay.

Important Points

Buffett contends that genuine originality is a myth and that creativity is not original. Every creative endeavor is impacted by earlier creations, and artists invariably find inspiration in their environment. The core of remixing is this process of taking, altering, and fusing preexisting elements.

Remixing is a spectrum: Remixing is a spectrum rather than a binary concept. Simple reproduction or copying is at one extreme, and remixes that drastically change the original content are at the other.

Because digital content is so easily copied, shared, and altered, the number of remixed works has skyrocketed, contributing to the acceleration of remix culture. Remixing is a common practice in online communities that have grown as a result of the internet.

Traditional ideas of authorship and ownership are challenged by remixing. Traditional notions of who is entitled to creative credit and who owns the rights to remixed works are called into question by the collaborative and transformative nature of remixing.

When remixing, ethical considerations are crucial: Remixing can be a potent creative outlet, but it's important to think about the moral ramifications, including copyright violations and cultural appropriation.

Important Results

Remixing is not a recent phenomenon; it has a long history. It has been around for centuries in a variety of forms, including literary adaptations and musical variations.

Remixing is a broad practice that includes a variety of artistic endeavors, such as mashups, sampling, adaptation, appropriation, and parody.

Many factors influence remixing: artists remix for a variety of reasons, such as commercial considerations, audience engagement, cultural commentary, and artistic expression.

The media landscape has been profoundly impacted by remixing, which has generated new business models in the entertainment sector, questioned conventional ideas of authorship, and blurred the boundaries between creator and consumer.

The ethical and legal issues surrounding remixing are complicated and multidimensional, and there are no simple solutions. Every case needs to be assessed separately, taking into account the particular circumstances and level of change that are involved.

List of references

Lawrence Lessig. Remix. Using the Hybrid Economy to Make Art and Business Successful. 2008 by Penguin Press.
Jonathan Zittrain. How to Stop the Internet and Its Future. Yale University Press, 2008.
Henry Jenkins. The intersection of new and old media is known as convergence culture. New York University Press, 2006.
Jonathan Sterne. MP3: What a Format Means. Duke University Press, 2012.
Mark Rose. Owners and Authors: The Development of Copyright. Press, Harvard University, 1993.

James Boyle. Software, Spleens, and Shamans: The Law and the Development of the Information Age. Press, Harvard University, 1996.

Siva Vaidhyanathan. The Rise of Intellectual Property and How It Endangers Creativity: Copyrights and Copywrongs. Press, New York University, 2001.

Tim Wu. The Master Switch: Information Empires' Ascent and Decline. Knopf, 2010.

Kenneth Goldsmith. Managing Language in the ***Digital Age:*** Uncreative Writing. 2011; Columbia University Press.

Kirby Ferguson. All of it is a remix. Vimeo, 2010.

This bibliography serves as a springboard for additional research into the intricate and intriguing realm of remix culture. We can learn more about the dynamics of originality, creativity, and intellectual property in the digital age by interacting with these and other sources.

Index

Is Everything a Remix? Asks the Remix Generation.

"The Remix Generation: Is Everything Remix?" by Eric Buffett examines how ubiquitous remixing is in modern culture and makes the case that all creative works are based on preexisting concepts, forms, and styles. The history of remixing, its different forms, and its effects on originality, creativity, and intellectual property are all covered in the book.

Index

The process of converting a work from one medium to another, like from a book to a movie or a video game to a television show, is called adaptation.

Taking preexisting sounds, images, or concepts from other sources and incorporating them into original works is known as appropriation.

Being the creator of a work is known as authorship.

Copyright: A legal privilege that shields an original work from unapproved use and is awarded to its creator.

Creativity: The capacity to generate novel and inventive concepts or objects.

The current era of technological advancement, known as the *"digital age,"* is defined by the pervasive use of computers and the internet.

Fair use is a concept in copyright law that permits restricted, unpermitted uses of copyrighted content for teaching, research, news reporting, criticism, and scholarship.

A mashup is an artistic creation that blends components from two or more previously created works.

Being novel and distinct is what is meant by originality.

A parody is a work that humorously mimics another work.

Presenting someone else's work as your own is known as plagiarism.

A remix is an artistic creation created by modifying or adapting preexisting works.

A society where remixing is a typical and accepted activity is known as a remix culture.

Sampling is the technique of using a section of an already-recorded song in a new composition.

Transformation is the process by which something is changed into another.

This index offers a thorough synopsis of the main ideas and vocabulary covered in "The **Remix Generation:** Is Everything a Remix?" Readers can learn more about the intricate and intriguing realm of remix culture by interacting with these concepts and examining the different examples offered in the book.

Adaptation, 1, 3, 7, 12, 19, 21, 25, 27, 32, 41, 43, 47, 52, 55, 62, 65, 69, 72, 75, 79, 81, 83, 86, 92, 95, 99, 102, 105, 108, 112, 115, 118, 121, 124, 127, 131, 134, 137, 141, 144, 147, 151, 154, 157, 161, 164, 167, 171, 174, 177, 181, 184, 187, 191, 194, 197, 201, 204

Appropriation, 2, 5, 8, 13, 17, 22, 26, 29, 33, 38, 42, 46, 51, 53, 57, 63, 66, 71, 73, 77, 82, 85, 89, 93, 96, 101, 103, 107, 111, 113, 117, 123, 125, 129, 132, 135, 139, 142, 145, 149, 152, 155, 159, 162, 165, 169, 172, 175, 179, 182, 185, 189, 192, 195, 199, 202

Authorship, 4, 9, 14, 18, 23, 28, 31, 34, 39, 44, 48, 52, 56, 61, 64, 68, 74, 78, 80, 84, 88, 91, 94, 98, 104, 106, 110, 114, 116, 120, 126, 128, 130, 133, 136, 140, 143, 146, 150, 153, 156, 160, 163, 166, 170, 173, 176, 180, 183, 186, 190, 193, 196, 200, 203

Copyright, 6, 10, 15, 20, 24, 27, 30, 35, 40, 45, 49, 53, 58, 60, 67, 70, 76, 79, 83, 87, 90, 97, 100, 109, 111, 119, 122, 131, 134, 138, 141, 148, 151, 158, 161, 168, 171, 178, 181, 188, 191, 198, 201

3, 7, 11, 16, 21, 25, 28, 32, 37, 41, 46, 50, 54, 59, 62, 65, 69, 72, 75, 79, 81, 83, 86, 92, 95, 99, 102, 105, 108, 112, 115, 118, 121, 124, 127, 131, 134, 137, 141, 144, 147, 151, 154, 157, 161, 164, 167, 171, 174, 177, 181, 184, 187, 191, 194, 197, 201, 204

1, 6, 10, 15, 19, 24, 28, 33, 37, 42, 46, 51, 54, 58, 66, 71, 73, 77, 82, 85, 89, 93, 96, 101, 103, 107, 111, 113, 117, 123, 1602, 165, 169, 172, 175, 179, 182, 185, 189, 192, 199, 202, Digital Age

Intellectual property, 6, 10, 15, 20, 24, 28, 33, 37, 42, 46, 51, 54, 58, 63, 66, 71, 73, 77, 82, 85, 89, 93, 96, 101, 103, 107, 111, 113, 117, 123, 125, Fair use, 9, 14, 18, 23, 28, 31, 34, 39, 44, 48, 52, 56, 61, 64, 68, 74, 78, 80, 84, 88, 91, 98, 104, 106, 110, 114, 116, 120, 126, 130, 133, 136, 140, 143, 146, 150, 153, 156, 160, 163, 166, 170, 176, 180, 183, 186, 190, 193, 196, 200, 203

www.ingramcontent.com/pod-product-compliance
Lightning Source LLC
Chambersburg PA
CBHW052138220526
45471CB00004B/1429